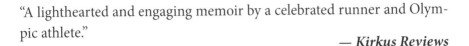

"A lighthearted and engaging memoir by a celebrated runner and Olympic athlete."
— *Kirkus Reviews*

"Abdi is a unique and competitive athlete. I had the chance to train with and compete against Abdi throughout almost three decades. Our discussions and interactions have always been fun-loving and ambitious. Abdi has a "go-big" approach to life and running, and now readers will get to experience his positive mindset firsthand. What an amazingly long and successful career Abdi has had!"

—**Meb Keflezighi**
2004 Olympic Marathon silver medalist,
2009 New York City Marathon winner,
2014 Boston Marathon winner

"Abdi is one of the most inspiring and decorated distance runners in the United States today, but also the most fun to be with at the races. He is a natural storyteller and a gritty performer, so put this book on your summer reading list for both motivation and entertainment."

—**Deena Kastor**
2004 Olympic Marathon bronze medalist,
American record holder in the marathon,
New York Times bestselling author of *Let Your Mind Run*

"I've always looked up to Abdi as a runner, as most do, but knowing Abdi, I more admire and want to emulate his carefree, happy-go-lucky, joy-filled nature. What is the point of becoming a world-beater athlete if you can't enjoy today? Abdi knows how to run with the best athletes in the world, but more importantly, he knows how to live a life full of joy, optimism, and love. I know that the words Abdi shares in *Abdi's World* will pass along his wisdom, fire, and joy to all that read them."

—**Ryan Hall**
Two-time Olympian;
American record holder in the half marathon

"Abdi's mentality is his foundation of youth. His huge smile and joy for life are his trademarks. His ability to read the race as it's developing and never back down are part of his competitive legacy. It's hard to imagine any one of those without the others. What a treat to read his secrets to success."

—**Mary Wittenberg,**
former president and CEO, New York Road Runners

"People often overlook just how difficult it is to achieve longevity in elite sports. Abdi has been entertaining at the very highest level for over 20 years. His energy lights up a room and those lucky enough to have met him leave with a little bit of his magic. You cannot fail to be inspired by Abdi's story, an authentic tale by someone who clearly cherishes running and life."

—**Gary Lough,**
distance coach, former professional middle-distance runner

"Abdi's desire and will have not changed. In really good athletes, they dance on that line of, How long can I do this? A lot lose the joy in it and it's not what it once was, and they have to work through that along with the physical relationship and how it sits in their lives. They exit without the joy. He's somebody who is always asking 'What am I getting ready for?' He always has a plan. He always, always, has been like that. With Abdi, as you will read in his life story, he still has the joy."

—**Mike Smith,**
director of track and field and cross country, Northern Arizona University, national cross country champions, 2017, 2018, 2020

"Abdi's always had that bold spirit and an ability to live up to his boldness. His character is alive and people in our baseball circle love it. His sport is a completely different world and we don't know a lot about that world, but we've always thought of him as an unbelievable competitor with great energy that's contagious. I wish more people had his attitude; his book will inspire readers to adopt it.

—**Shelley Duncan,**
University of Arizona baseball All-American,
six-year Major League Baseball veteran

ABDI'S WORLD

The Black Cactus on Life, Running, and Fun

Abdi Abdirahman

with Myles Schrag

FOREWORD BY MO FARAH

Soulstice
PUBLISHING
books with *soul* • Flagstaff, AZ

Abdi's World: The Black Cactus on Life, Running, and Fun

ISBN: 978-1-7331887-8-4 (paperback)
ISBN: 978-1-7331887-9-1 (e-book)
Library of Congress Control Number: 2021907837

Cover designed by Lindy Martin
Interior designed by Katherine Lloyd
Copyediting by Julie Hammonds
Proofreading by Claudine Taillac
Editorial support by Nancy Schrag

Printing by Sheridan Books, Chelsea, Michigan, USA

Cover photo © Kevin Morris. Abdi Abdirahman, on February 29, 2020, after qualifying for his fifth Olympic team at the US Olympic Team Marathon Trials in Atlanta, Georgia.

Soulstice Publishing
PO Box 791
Flagstaff, AZ 86002
(928) 814-8943
connect@soulsticepublishing.com
www.soulsticepublishing.com

10 9 8 7 6 5 4 3 2 1

CONTENTS

FOREWORD

People know Abdi Abdirahman for being eccentric and funny. Sure, that is true: to say Abdi marches to the beat of his own drum is an understatement.

He's also incredibly stubborn. It took me several years to convince him to join me and other Somali-born runners for altitude-training camps in Ethiopia. Even when he did decide to participate, he couldn't give a reason for not having come years before. It was as though one day he just decided the time was right, and so he booked his flight.

Once he finally arrived in Addis Ababa, it quickly became clear we had found the missing piece to our puzzle. He gave the training group a shift in energy—Abdi knows when to push and when to rest. He knows when it's time to work and when it's time to play. I don't think most distance runners do. Actually, I'm not sure most people do. Many of us try to control everything, and I think one of his best traits is knowing when to let things slide and when action is needed. He accepts good news and bad news equally and moves forward from there.

There's lots I could make fun of Abdi for—and I do. For being the "old man" of the running world, for speaking Somali poorly, for forgetting his keys or a meeting time, for being resistant about returning to Africa. Instead, I'll tell you what you discover when you get to know him.

He's a fantastic training partner. For somebody who seems so laid back and uninterested in the details of training, his tenacity is unmatched when it's time to get down to work. If it wasn't, I assure you that he wouldn't have been able to make five Olympic teams.

His longevity is amazing. The guy can flat-out run. By the time I won gold medals in the 5000m and 10,000m at the 2010 European Track and Field Championships, Abdi Abdirahman had already been in three Olympics. I first met Abdi when I was 16 years old, running the junior race at the 2000 World Cross Country Championships in Vilamoura, Portugal. He was a role model for me then, and he still is.

He doesn't have enemies. He talks with the same respect and dignity to everyone he meets and can very quickly be joking and having a laugh with people.

He's intelligent. Yes, he likes to goof around, so much so that some people think he has no common sense. But I'll let you in on a little secret: the guy is smart. By that, I mean he's sharp when it comes to training and race tactics, and I mean he's thoughtful when you talk to him about the world and what he values as a person. Abdi doesn't speak out as much as a lot of us do about his athletic feats or about events and issues. He prefers to lead by example and respect others' opinions. We all take notice of his approach to life.

I'm excited that his book will give you the chance to get to know him as well as I've gotten to know him through the years. I think you'll enjoy learning about what makes Abdi such a special guy.

It's Abdi's world and we're all just living in it.

Sir Mo Farah
Addis Ababa, Ethiopia
February 2021

PREFACE

My running friends tease me about being an "old man." I could take that to mean I've got tons of wisdom to share (maybe true) or I can't keep up with them anymore (definitely not true) or maybe just that people are comfortable and like to have fun around me (definitely true).

I am quite sure that nobody loves to run more than I do. That's a good thing, because it's been my profession my whole adult life, and it's taken me to the Olympics, World Championships, major marathons, track meets, and road races all over the world in competition.

I figure from age 19 until I'm writing this just weeks after my 44th birthday, I've covered more than 100,000 miles. I can't say for sure, because I don't always pay attention to my Garmin GPS watch and I've never kept a training log. I'd bet I have thousands and thousands of miles still in me too, whether I use them in big races or on remote trails.

You'll discover that running is far from the only thing I enjoy in life. I'd say the fact that I'm beating competitors 10 or 20 years younger than me is partly because at the end of the day, I don't take myself or my sport—my job—too seriously. I'm grateful that running has given me the opportunity to experience more of the life I want. I like hanging out with friends on a weekend in Telluride, Colorado. I like trying out my second language, Swahili, with unsuspecting young Kenyan runners. I'm always ready to try new foods, find a new Prada shirt to wear, or drink an afternoon coffee when I'm in Ethiopia. I read the BBC online to know more about what's going on in the world—a world it's been my honor to experience through running.

If you're picking up this book, you probably know me because I've been in this sport for the whole 21st century. Maybe you've watched me run major marathons such as New York City and Boston. On Leap Day, February 29, 2020, I became the first American distance runner to qualify for five Olympic teams. But I hope when you finish this book, you'll have enjoyed it in part because my life is not defined by my running career—it's defined by the choices I make, the way I look at the world each day, and the people I surround myself with.

I call this book *Abdi's World* because I've always tried to be unconventional—pushing the pace when I can and enjoying the effort and challenge along the way. Now I'm inviting you to keep up with me and be part of my world for a little while. Getting up every morning is fun to me, especially when I know I'm going for a run. I want you to experience that joy in training and in the choices you make each day. The short version of this book is pretty simple: don't take yourself too seriously. But stick with me for the longer version; it's more fun—and maybe, just maybe, it's not quite as simple as I make it look.

I can tell you without regret that sometimes when I push the pace, the pack runs me down, but I always give it my best effort. I may be the "old man" on the marathon circuit these days, but I plan to keep making the most of my time on the roads and in life until I truly am an old man . . . whatever that term even means!

If you pick this up thinking you're going to get all the best training tips, you'll probably be disappointed—or maybe you'll discover that applying my approach improves your own workouts and races. Either way, you may find out things about me or yourself that are meaningful to you. I really hope so.

So here's the way this book is going to work: I'll take you through my experience with every Summer Olympics of the 21st century. Why? Because I have qualified for five of the six of them thus far—and I learned just as much from the one I missed as any of the others. In each of the six parts of the book, you'll get a mix of my thoughts on the world, running, and living. In the process, you'll also discover my personal story, not just in professional distance running but also growing up in Mogadishu, Somalia; Mombasa, Kenya; and Tucson, Arizona. I've even included sections called "Chasing Abdi," in which friends, reporters, and podcasters share fun memories. This turned out to be one of the most enjoyable tasks in writing the book.

We're all chasing something. I know some of us are trying to run down demons, and that can be exhausting. I prefer to focus on pursuing the best that the world has to offer. That can sometimes be difficult, but the results are worth pushing the pace.

I'm not saying I have all the answers; no way is that true. Even if I haven't always known the path I should take, I've persevered when I have a goal in mind, and I've done my best to stay true to core values that point me in the right direction. Come join me now as I share some of what I've learned in a very blessed life. Welcome to *Abdi's World*.

HIDE-AND-SEEK

Kadimay, kadimay, kadim.
Kadimay, kadimay, kow.
Kadimay, kadimay, labo.
Kadimay, kadimay, sadex.

In the few seconds it took to hear six of my friends shout out those words, five other friends and I had already scattered throughout the neighborhood to look for a hiding place. Darkness was descending on a mild Mogadishu summer evening. Papaya trees were waving in the salty sea breeze, casting shadows on what little sunlight remained. Most of the adults who were hanging around outside a couple hours earlier had gone inside. Maybe they had samosas filled with beef and potatoes for dinner. If they had a television set, they would be watching the news. Only a few lounged outside, having a tea or watching us kids laugh and play and tease each other.

This game was basically like cops and robbers, and it was one of the best parts of what I remember as a pretty ideal childhood in Somalia. What 13-year-old boy doesn't love running around with his friends playing what is basically a cross country version of team hide-and-seek? We had the whole neighborhood to ourselves. No adults cared if we ran through the sandy alleys and pathways between their stucco and stone houses, even if we ran into their shirts and sheets hanging on the clothesline when we tried to avoid getting tagged.

Once the seekers finished counting, "*kow . . . labo . . . sadex* (one . . .

two . . . three)," we knew six sets of eyes had popped open. They were on the chase for the rest of us, whether or not we had managed to find a place to hide.

This is meant to be a fast-paced game. Because you don't have much time to hide, the team that counts is usually able to snuff out the hiders before they can get too far away from home base, which for us sat in the dirt-road intersection in the middle of our simple neighborhood in the Somali capital city.

Quickly, one boy found another boy behind a house and tagged him. The fastest boy of all saw an opening where the base was exposed and became the first on my team to safety. Another friend of mine ran barefoot. He lost a toenail to one of many stray rocks in our sandy yards, but still reached home base untouched before he yowled in pain.

While one of my teammates found refuge behind a chicken coop about the distance of a soccer pitch away, and another assessed the situation from behind a trash can, the other team started to spread out to find us three remaining hiders. If just one more of us could reach home without getting tagged, we would get to hide again rather than switch to becoming the seekers.

Some of my friends preferred to protect the base, but I always liked being on the run. It wasn't that I liked hiding more than seeking so much as I preferred running away and outlasting the other team. I liked being chased! I wasn't the fastest, but I could go forever. And so I did. I took off, four or five blocks away, past sleeping dogs and backyard flower and tomato gardens. Everyone knew this was my strategy, but no one knew what direction I would go. And even if they did see which way I went, they didn't know which way I would come back. That was considered nuts by most of my friends—way too much work. But I loved it. Not only was I valuable to my team, my strategy even gave me time to daydream about soccer and what my mom was making for dinner while I caught my breath and plotted my return route. Others were caught or safe in the first minute. I'd be on my own for 10 minutes.

I was being chased—but I was the one in control.

Still, I had to be tactical. Come back too soon and I lose my advantage;

stay too long and everybody else was either safe or captured, meaning the other guys could guard home base and wait rather than pursue. Then I'd be too late to help my team.

I sprinted to the big house south of the base, and as I turned to look over my shoulder, I saw one boy running after me, pushing me farther from the center. I kept going and he slowed to a walk, content to have kept me away from safety, conserving his energy. I looped around the rut-filled streets until I was on the north side of the neighborhood. Surely seven or eight minutes had passed. I worked my way toward the inner circle, making sure not to be seen. Soon I was 50 meters away from home base and standing beside a tiny house, angled just right to see the whole scene.

One of the guys on my team had left the coop and was getting pushed farther away from the goal. He was sure to be caught. The other held onto his hiding spot behind the trash can, but two seekers were closing in. Three others were following my initial path, scouting the alleys and road to the south. They had to be at least 75 meters away from the station.

This was my time. I bolted for the goal. Within seconds, one boy heard me.

"Abdi!" he yelled, pointing toward me. His teammates joined in: "Abdi! *Wakaas*! (Abdi! There!)"

The chase was on! I had four boys after me from all directions—and once my two teammates were caught, I had two more chasers join the fun of trying to run me down. One boy near the trash can had heard the commotion and reversed course to come after me. He was closer than the three boys now running toward the goal from the south—he was their last hope to stop me. We had two safe and three tagged; I would be the difference one way or the other. My pursuer was chugging as fast as he could but got bogged down in a soft, sandy spot. I, on the other hand, was in full stride. With 25 meters to go, I knew I would be our third player to reach the goal.

My teammates were chanting my name: "Abdi! Abdi! Abdi!" I ran as fast as I could. I might as well have been heading down the homestretch of the 10,000 meters at the 1988 Olympics in Seoul, South Korea.

It was the fall of 1990. Little did I know that in a few months my family would be forced to leave this idyllic spot and that I wouldn't see my native country again for almost 25 years—and that I would never play this game with my friends again.

Part I
Sydney 2000

A LESSON
IN POSSIBILITIES

"Abdi has tremendous pride to be an American.
He's not a Somali running for the U.S.
No. He's an American."

—Dave Murray, my friend and coach

1

ALONE IN
THE CAFETERIA

I know exactly when and where my career as a professional runner began: the Pima Community College cafeteria in Tucson, Arizona, fall of 1995.

I was a freshman and would eat lunch there with my buddies. Some of them I knew from my year and a half at Tucson High School, but many of them were PCC athletes I had just met. We could waste a *lot* of time there after class, but eventually, they all would get up to leave. Everybody. They had to get ready for fall baseball workouts, early-season basketball training, or cross country or soccer practice. The guys teased me and said I should join them, but training sounded like a lot of work.

Besides, I hadn't played sports at Tucson High, so making a college team didn't seem like an option. Some of my best friends were baseball players, and I liked watching the weird American sport, but no one starts swinging a bat at age 18 and hits curveballs. Basketball? I was 5 feet, 10 inches tall, and weighed 130 pounds . . . if I exaggerated a little bit. I would get crushed going in for a layup. Like any kid growing up in Somalia and Kenya, I would play soccer, pretending I was in the Italian Serie A and emulating the older kids in the local league. I was a decent soccer player, I guess, but it was more than three years since I'd been in a refugee camp kicking a ball. At least that was running with a purpose: put the ball in the goal or stop the other guys from putting the ball in the goal. But I seriously doubted after so long that I would be good enough to try out.

That left running, which seemed like the most work of all. Did I really want to spend an hour each afternoon running across town with some coach yelling at me? I stayed in the cafeteria, though I hated to sit there alone.

When spring semester came around, I was increasingly restless. I was taking a full load of freshman intro classes and making some money as a sales clerk and stock boy at Mervyn's in the home fashion department. But I wanted to meet more people, and I wanted something else to do besides work and school. I started to think seriously about whether I could make the cross country team in the fall, when I would be a sophomore. One of my best friends was a pretty decent cross country runner and steeplechaser. More than anybody, Bogibo Yohannes kept on me. He lived in the same apartment complex as I did and had plenty of chances to plant the seed in my head. "You could help the team," Bogi said, over and over and over.

The real inspiration to take action came when I drove across town to Drachman Stadium at the University of Arizona for an early-season all-comers track meet to watch my PCC friends compete. I'd love to tell you I saw photos of great Wildcat runners through the years—names like George Young, Ed Mendoza, Aaron Ramirez, Matt Giusto, Marc Davis, and Martin Keino—and decided then and there, I want to put in the hard work and dedication to be part of that legacy. The truth is, I didn't see any U of A Hall of Fame plaques on campus that day, and I wouldn't have known who any of them were even if they had walked right in front of me and waved as I watched the meet.

The person who caught my attention was a guy from Central Arizona College who finished almost a lap behind the rest of the field in the 3000-meter run. I figured if he could run collegiate track, then so could I. This may have been twisted logic, and it was less than aspirational, but it wasn't the last time I would receive inspiration from odd places. Thank you, unnamed runner for the Central Arizona Vaqueros! I think I probably owe you a beer.

The next day, Bogi took me to Pima head coach Jim Mielke's office and introduced us. I shook Coach Mielke's hand and told him I'd like to try out for the cross country team in the fall. He saw no reason to wait. "Come back tomorrow and join us for track practice," he said.

I had no running shoes, so I showed up for the workout in Rockport work boots and jean shorts. By the end of that five-mile run, the only person on the team who had beaten me was John Landsa. And he had to outsprint me at the end. I had secured an invitation to join the Aztecs for the rest of the spring track season. Fortunately, that invitation also came with a more suitable pair of running shoes.

Nick Farmer was the distance coach at Pima. He saw enough in me to devote time to helping me improve. My fitness came along quickly, and soon I ran my first track race, a 5000 meters. I had no idea what to do. I'd sprint 200 meters, then jog 200 meters. But I ran a pretty respectable time, about a 15:05, with that unusual approach. I kept running 1500m and 5000m races at meets. Figuring out how to pace myself was a fun challenge. In some ways, it even reminded me of playing hide-and-seek in Somalia nearly a decade earlier. How fast could I go and still have some gas left to expend at the finish line? What is it like to maneuver around guys without getting boxed in?

I didn't answer any of these questions with great certainty, but I was fairly successful those first few months of running—I even came close to winning a couple times. I am competitive when I really get into something, whether it's a board game or talking trash with friends or a footrace. Mostly, I was just grateful to be spending more time with my best Tucson friends. It was also pretty cool to discover I was decent at something I assumed that I hated. Going to practices and meets was a whole new experience. This was an opportunity to do something with myself besides finishing my schoolwork and selling people sheets and towels.

Running made me happy. I didn't have grand ambitions about doing it for a living. Happiness was its own reward, and while life can feel more complicated when you get older, I haven't forgotten to notice the joy in even the simplest moment. When I put on a USA singlet at the Olympics,

I can still distinctly remember how much I enjoyed putting on the orange and blue PCC singlet that first spring.

$$\mathscr{F} \; \mathscr{F} \; \mathscr{F}$$

When track season ended, I continued running. Coach Farmer gave us summer workouts to do on our own, and I was a diligent student. Cross country season was coming. I enjoyed getting out each morning before the desert heat settled in. This meant that in August, when we started cross country workouts, I was in decent shape, ready to see whether I might be able to medal at races. My PCC coaches and teammates encouraged me to think big. Could I finish in the top 25 at meets with more than 100 runners? Top 10? They sure thought so. For me, I just wondered how to make sure I didn't get trampled at the starting line.

One day I was doing a workout by myself at Gates Pass, running past miles of saguaro cactuses and over the Tucson Mountains west of town. The U of A cross country team happened to be there too, and their coach, Dave Murray, noticed me. He asked me if I was running for anybody.

"Yeah," I said. "For Pima. I'm on the cross country team."

He smiled. "You look really good."

That simple exchange meant a lot to me, and as I kept improving, the possibility of continuing to run after I got my associate's degree at Pima really sounded good. When we practiced, our routes sometimes overlapped with those chosen by the U of A team. The campuses were only 10 minutes away, but like coaches on most distance running teams, our coaches wanted to assign workouts that were scenic and away from city traffic. That meant we would sometimes run into the Wildcats on trails in the mountains that surround Tucson on all sides.

I have to admit, this wasn't always on accident. I wanted Coach Murray and his runners to see me. If given the opportunity, I would take the same route as those guys for a few miles. Coach Murray never said much, but he would wave and say hello when we crossed paths. I later found out that he felt the same way—he wanted me to see his team working out and consider running for him next year. We sometimes say it was love at first sight. Considering he's been my coach ever since I started at U of A in 1997 and through six Olympic cycles, I'd say we make a good team. I can't imagine having gone on this journey this long with anybody else.

I was running well in cross country and then track. I even won some races, including two Arizona Community College Athletic Conference titles, but my times weren't impressive compared to many top high school runners that Coach Murray could have gone after. Still, he started recruiting me and invited me to make an official campus visit.

CHASING ABDI

"When you travel to races all the time, you see a lot of the same competitors. Abdi was one of those people who was more authentic, not in it for the ends but for love of the sport. He found out what running was at Pima. He didn't even know what it was. It was a bonus thing. He wasn't 'using it.'

"He's successful and financially, running has been good to him, but I think when you start that way, you're always going to finish that way. If your parents are hardcore runners, you're always going to come from that angle. The way he started was part of the way he interacted with it, and that was appealing to me."

—Anthony Famiglietti, Olympic steeplechaser

Do you ever stop and consider how lucky you are to come across some of the people you meet in life? Here I was getting recruited by Coach Murray to be part of his national-class program, located in a city where top athletes such as 800m world record holder Wilson Kipketer happened to be training. And just a year earlier, I was telling my friends I hated running.

I feel like my life is one continuous series of these encounters. This good fortune didn't start with Kipketer. Or Bogi. Or coaches like Dave

Murray, Jim Mielke, and Nick Farmer. But these friends and mentors influenced my next five years in profound ways that changed my life forever. I may not have started running until I was 19 years old, but almost since the day I began doing it, I feel like I've been training for the biggest races in the world. Inspiration and support are all around me when I'm open to looking for them—and even sometimes when I'm not.

My family fled Somalia when I was 13. We arrived in Malindi, Kenya, on a boat from Kismayo, Somalia: my mom and dad, me, two brothers, two sisters, and then my baby sister, who was born right after we arrived in Malindi. Along with hundreds of other refugees, we didn't know where to go once we reached shore, but an Italian woman saw that my pregnant mother needed help, and she got them to the hospital and the rest of us to a hotel with food. Her name was Giannina. Why we were fortunate enough to have her find my family in a time of desperation, I don't know. All I know is I'm here today in part because of Giannina.

None of us get the same start in life as others. That's just not the way the world works. It's why one of the best things we all can do for each other is to show compassion for each other, give each other the benefit of the doubt, and accept that we don't know what others are going through at any given moment.

My parents managed to get us out of a country in civil war and relocate us to the United States, where I was able to get an education and pursue a running career. I'm eternally grateful for that. I remember being a 16-year-old at Tucson High School. I'd been in the country for a few weeks. I didn't speak English. I felt alone every time I left our little home in southeast Tucson for even a few minutes. Inside, I was safe. Outside it, I was lost.

I learned early on that to live in a new place and meet new people, I had to be resilient and aware of my surroundings and be willing to trust others. This is difficult to do in a new language in a new country, and sometimes that trust in others is misplaced. But I'd rather take that chance and be open to the world. Maybe experiencing all of this as a child is a blessing of sorts. My parents had to learn American life after being set in their ways. I had the luxury, if you want to call it that, of learning to go with the flow. I feel like that still serves me well.

I have gotten to know many African expatriates during my running career. Lopez Lomong had to run for days to escape captivity as a "Lost Boy" of Sudan before eventually carrying the American flag during Opening Ceremonies of the 2008 Beijing Olympics. Guor Maker lost dozens of family members in the Sudanese civil war before South Sudan became a country. He ran the Olympic marathon in 2012 without a country and in 2016 with one. Diane Nukuri decided to seek asylum from violence in Burundi during a meet in Canada. Mo Farah, Hassan Mead, Bashir Abdi, and many other friends were born in Somalia. Some were separated from their families or relocated many times, eventually to settle somewhere else in the world. There are many more stories like this, and they remind me that we never fully know what other people have experienced. While I don't intend to compare my life with others, I know I haven't endured nearly as much struggle and tragedy as some other African-born runners and other people around the world. I just want to share my story when possible, and listen to others' when they are ready to share theirs.

As I considered the opportunity to run at an NCAA Division I university in the Pac-10 Conference, I didn't yet know that I was about to meet two other Africans—one from Kenya and one from Eritrea—who would become important influences on me for years to come.

2

BEARING DOWN
AT RIM ROCK

My second year at Pima Community College flew by quickly. No question I was improving—and not just by avoiding getting trampled. Coach Farmer had me running intense workouts, and I devoured them. I was running from the front and forcing the field to chase me. At the National Junior College Athletic Association cross country meet, I took second place. In the spring, I was runner-up again in the 5000m at the NJCAA track and field championships. It felt good, and while I wouldn't say it came easy, I definitely had confidence that I was where I needed to be to take a shot at the next level of competition.

Ultimately, I signed with the University of Arizona. We had a modest ceremony, at my academic advisor's office down the hall from the PCC cafeteria where it all began. It just felt right: two more years in town, on trails and training routes I already knew, only this time at a state university with more than 30,000 students and a running tradition steeped in history. Most importantly, Coach Murray was leading me.

That may have seemed like an easy recruiting job by him, but NCAA Division I is a big leap for a runner from NJCAA. Giving out scholarships is a major investment for an athletic program, and in sports like track and cross country, coaches often offer partial scholarships so they can provide assistance to more athletes. Even at a big university like Arizona, track and cross country coaches don't have the money that football and basketball coaches do to entice recruits. Coach Murray had 12.6 scholarships to parcel out across 21 men's track events and cross country runners.

At the end of the day, I was a good junior college runner, but my personal bests were around 31 minutes in the 10,000m and 15 minutes in the 5000m. I'd only been running for a year. His assistant coaches thought he was crazy. Still, Coach Murray believed I could be a positive impact on the program. He offered me a full ride.

"I hate to say I was influenced by a stereotype, but here was this skinny African guy," said Murray to *Deadspin* writer Sarah Barker in 2016. "He looked like he could run. I had a good feeling about Abdi. I took a chance, no question about it, but right from the get-go he was running really good times."

From my first cross country races as a Wildcat in 1997, I was running with the leaders from other teams. I actually won my first two races, the Jammin' Invitational in Brea, California, and the Aztec Invitational in San Diego. Coach Murray told me not to start thinking I had figured the sport out, though. The season was young, and we still had the rugged Pac-10 Conference and a tough West Regional to get through.

$$\mathcal{F} \; \mathcal{F} \; \mathcal{F}$$

At the University of Arizona, I was in a whole different universe. I felt like I was a superstar, and at the same time I didn't feel superior to anybody else. I don't know if that makes sense, but I want to explain it.

Of course I had been on the U of A campus a couple times in the four years since my family had moved to Tucson. As in any university town, field trips and local events give anyone in the community a reason to be on campus from time to time. But now I was representing that big university. Athletes from other sports were starting to recognize me at the McKale Center training facilities. Like at Pima, I enjoyed hanging out with the baseball players, and at Arizona that included future major leaguer Shelley Duncan. Shelley told me I had a baseball player's "bravado." Once I was messing around playing football with the baseball team. I could run the deep route, but I couldn't catch the ball. It didn't stop me from talking smack to them though.

Students would point at me and say hello when I walked past the palm trees and saguaros on the quad and past the beautiful brick Old Main building. I really enjoyed the attention, and I'd say hello to everybody I saw. It was like I had thousands of friends around at any given time. After years of not feeling confident with the language or the culture, I was finally feeling more at ease with both, and at the same time I was experiencing success at something others could see. A lot of transitions were coming together at once, and for the first time I was feeling comfortable with who I was.

Coming to an American high school midway through my junior year had been really hard for me. I was good at learning English, but I was starting from square one and trying to make friends while doing it. I felt awkward all the time. Kids were always trying to be cool, and it seemed like getting in fights was one way to do it. I didn't want any part of that. I didn't know how to approach people in general, so I just limited my interactions. I ended up being a shy teenager, even though people laugh now when I say that.

Academics were hard at high school and at Pima too, but classes were smaller and the assignments were manageable, so I survived. At Arizona, I took academics seriously, mostly because I wanted to stay eligible, to be honest. I did enjoy some courses. I chose to major in retail and consumer studies. Ever since coming to the United States, I had liked seeing high-quality clothes and colorful displays in storefronts. And here I was getting the chance to study how top brands make their products and how store managers try to influence our buying choices.

I learned something then that has always stayed with me. At the mall, the most ordinary items can look incredible surrounded with bright colors and just the right lighting. Put a Gucci logo on a shoe, put intense lighting on it, rotate it in a circular display case, and people crave it. They don't realize that they are seeing it as perfect as it will ever be. When they take home those shoes, or a purse or a shirt, whatever it is, they won't have that same lighting and it won't seem as wonderful as when they first laid eyes on it. I still like nice things and probably always will. But I think about that a lot—something we desire is never as satisfying once we get it as we think it's going to be when we don't yet have it. It works both ways, though. When we get something we don't want, like bad news or a poorly made product, the effect is not as bad as we think it is going to be. Depending on how you look at it, I guess that can sound either cynical or hopeful, but to me it's just an honest and helpful way to look at the world.

I always say the University of Arizona was the two best years of my life, and the main reason for that was my track and cross country teammates. I wasn't trying to *be* anybody or be better than anybody else (except when I was running, of course!). It's always great to find out you love doing something you're pretty good at, but it was more than just running that I enjoyed. I lived off campus at the "Cross Country House" with a bunch of great guys, and we really cared about each other. My teammates made me feel comfortable and loved. They introduced me to new friends and new experiences. If I said something wrong, they wouldn't make fun of me. Even if they did laugh at me, I knew they didn't care. They'd correct me—usually in a kind way—which then made me less self-conscious and more willing to take chances and talk to other people myself.

My roommates both years were Jeremy Lyon, a steeplechaser, and Akim Akrami, a sprinter; they were the best. I remember Jeremy coming home one day and telling me he had met the love of his life. He had asked her to get a soda with him and she said yes. It sounded so cheesy, but he was sincere. They did later get married and have been together throughout his distinguished career in the U.S. Navy. Relationships with guys like that have stayed with me ever since.

As much as I enjoyed the Cross Country House, I still felt most at home when I was running. Coach Murray was never considered a high-mileage coach by any of his athletes; we rarely topped 70 miles a week in workouts. He believed in hills and intensity and avoided junk miles. I think that worked especially well for me. I hadn't been running very long, so it allowed me to ease into figuring out what I could do. Also, it gave me a chance to work on improving my speed, since that was my weakest area. For instance, he would have me do 12 to 16 400-meter runs and finish with negative splits. Coach Murray would say, "There is a time to train and a time to strain," meaning you couldn't put maximum effort into every workout without burning out. He called tempo runs "control runs," and taught me to focus on how my body was feeling and to maintain a tough pace for long stretches.

When we started racing against Pac-10 schools, the competition was intense. I couldn't have picked a more challenging place to get educated about the sport. I looked forward to going to meets because I'd get to talk with a runner from Eritrea who was killing it at UCLA and another guy from Kenya who was leading Washington State University. They were both about two years older than me and seemed a lot more mature even than that.

They probably thought I was hyper, because they were both reserved and quiet, but I made sure to initiate conversation with them when I met them in person at the 1997 Pac-10 Conference Cross Country Championships. It was comforting just having the chance to see other Africans and know they understood what it was like to figure out a new country and enjoy the opportunity to run and go to school. Plus, Mebrahtom Keflezighi and Bernard Kipchirchir Lagat seemed pretty cool, like they were two guys I'd like to get to know better.

I had communicated a little with Kip, as Lagat's teammates called him, on the phone and in those early days of email, but we didn't meet in person until that conference championship at Stanford. Kip told me what stood out immediately when we spoke was that my Swahili was almost as good as his. We talked a little about Africa, but otherwise we were there to run, so maybe a hello during team warmups and a short chat on the podium. Kip won that day. Meb, as Keflezighi was called, had won the year before, and I would win conference the next year.

Meb was the national cross country champion for UCLA in 1997, and Kip was third for WSU. I placed seventh, just ahead of two Stanford runners, Nathan Nutter and Brad Hauser, giving the Pac-10 five runners in the top 10. The next spring, though, I was conference champion in the 5000m (14:01.01) and 10,000m (28:36.16). About halfway through the 10,000, I opened up a huge lead. Over the last half mile, Meb was coming. He kept closing the gap and just about nipped me at the end, but I held on. That was the type of rivalry the three of us had. Back and forth. I won some and lost some, but I always enjoyed the challenge, and I truly was happy for Meb and Kip when they had good days. That combination of loving my teammates, loving my opponents, and doing my best each time only made my love for the sport keep building.

CHASING ABDI

Excerpt from "Brief Chat: Abdirahman and Lagat," an article by Peter Gambaccini in *Runner's World*, April 4, 2012.

Peter: Because you have the long record of racing frequently and with great success and all that consistency, we might think of you as a guy who doesn't have motivational problems. But have there ever been times when you find Abdi to actually be a source of motivation for you when you have some doldrums, if you have any doldrums?

Bernard Lagat: Yes, absolutely. Abdi is not just a training partner, he is like a brother, and so whenever I have a problem, I need to tell it to somebody. He is the guy that I want to talk to right away. I just ring Abdi, or Abdi drives over to my house, we'll talk, I'll go to his house, we'll talk, or we can meet at Starbucks or somewhere and I'll talk with Abdi. So Abdi has been a source of inspiration for me. I've had ups and downs, and a true friend will actually show up at a time that you need, and that person will always be with you, and he will never leave you alone, and that has been Abdi. Every time I have something to tell him, I just feel like I'm down, I just talk to him. People can look at you and be like, "Okay, that guy, he doesn't have any problems, he always runs good." But there are a few times, I'm not running as good, I'm not feeling good in training, and what can I do to do this, and Abdi is always there, and we've been like that.

I thought I had my own national title a few weeks later at the NCAA Outdoor Championships in Buffalo, New York. I went into the 10,000m with one of the fastest times, but Stanford controlled the race, outkicked all of us over the final 600 meters, and easily swept the top three places: Brad Hauser nipped his twin brother Brent and Nutter by a second, while Meb was seven seconds back in fourth and I was seven seconds behind Meb, sixth in 28:46.36. So two nights later I decided I was going to set the pace and take control of the 5000. I opened up a 100-meter lead that I thought was insurmountable, but Colorado's Adam Goucher stalked me and pulled away over the last half lap. I held on for second, four seconds ahead of Meb.

In a strange way, Adam and I forever became entwined in running lore in fall 1998. He was well known at that point. He was runner-up at the national cross country meet to University of Arizona star Martin Keino as a freshman and had been fourth in 1997, when Meb won. This was his last chance to win a race that people felt he was destined to win after that breakout performance his very first collegiate season. But the field was stacked. Meb had finished his eligibility, but Bernard, the Hauser twins from Stanford, former junior college champion Julius Mwangi of Butler, Arkansas' Sean Kaley, Matthew Downin of Wisconsin, and others had just as much interest in winning. I was definitely in that confident group, and this was my senior year too.

The 1998 NCAA National Cross Country Championships were held at Rim Rock Farm, a beautiful course outside of Lawrence, Kansas, built by longtime University of Kansas coach Bob Timmons. As you enter the property, you see silhouettes on the bluffs that show the distinctive strides of famous KU runners such as Wes Santee, Billy Mills, and Jim Ryun, all of whom happened to be in attendance that day. I was starting to learn more running history, so this was a big deal. The movie *Running Brave*, about Mills' life, is still one of my favorites. Watching him come back in the 1964 Tokyo Olympics 10,000m to win gold always inspires me.

I was determined to assert myself and took the lead in the first mile of the 10K course in 4:33, with 254 runners nipping at my heels. Adam was right there with me. I didn't know it at the time, but Adam and his Colorado teammates were having their season chronicled by Chris Lear in what would become a best-selling book, *Running with the Buffaloes*. Here's how Lear described us:

> Although only 141 pounds, he looks enormous next to Abdirahman. Goucher powers along, every step a contraction and expansion of swollen muscles that have hardened for this task. With his skeleton-like frame, Abdirahman merely floats. While Goucher is an American SUV, gobbling up fuel from a massive tank, Abdirahman moves with the clean efficiency of a sleek two-door roadster. Abdirahman's engine purrs as his elbows cock back, and his willowy legs glide forward, always forward. He has no backkick, no wasted motion, and looks as if he is out for a Sunday stroll. Only the obvious exertion of those around Abdirahman gives him away (p. 243).

Jonathan Gault of LetsRun.com went back in 2020 and watched Fox SportsNet's broadcast of the race. He had some pretty hilarious commentary underneath screen captures of the day, and he also made sure to mention my stride: "The film quality may be Zapruder-like," he wrote about the 22-year-old footage, "but Abdi Abdirahman's form is instantly recognizable. I'd know that high, gently rolling arm carriage anywhere!" I laugh at this. People say I'm a heel striker or a shuffler. I guess. I think I'm an efficient runner, but I just run by feel. Running is simply putting one foot in front of the other, and I'm pretty good at that. I've never tried to change my form, because I think it would lead to an injury.

I wasn't quite so eloquent as Lear or Gault in my description of the battle when I was interviewed before the race, but I think my explanation described my approach to running pretty well. Fox SportsNet broadcast it early on to race viewers: "There's no strategy. This is not like a football game or a soccer game, the coach will tell you to pick a play. It's not that kind of game. This is running," I smiled. "Whoever can last long will win the race. That's it . . . Whoever runs fast, whoever is stronger, wins. That's it."

And then the announcer summed it up: "The native Somalian with a simple philosophy: the last guy standing."

Just after the halfway mark at Rim Rock, there's a covered bridge. Kaley took the lead coming out of the bridge, but I answered the challenge and led the charge up John Lawson Hill. I can't say this was my strategy going in. I just felt good and wanted to drop guys. Only Goucher, Kaley, and Lagat went with me, so I achieved that. By the time we reached the four-mile mark, it was just Adam and me, with ominous Billy Mills Hill looming about a mile away. We were side by side. I usually like to attack hills, even when they're really steep like that one. This time, though, I didn't have an answer. Goucher broke the race open over the final mile and won in 29:26. I placed second in 29:49, with Mwangi and Downin third and fourth in 30:00. Kip held on for seventh in 30:20. In his postrace interview, Adam described it this way: "By listening to his breathing, I felt like maybe he was a little more tired than me. Possibly. From the time we broke away, maybe four miles, to the time we got to the top of Billy Mills Hill, we were just feeling each other out getting ready for the surge to the end."

When I read Lear's book later, I felt like he tried to make it sound like I was the guy standing in Adam's way: "At 1K, Abdirahman puts in a little surge, getting into his rhythm, and the pack follows," Lear wrote. "A minute later, Abdirahman surges again. Goucher is not surprised; he has raced him before, and he knows this is how Abdirahman runs (242)."

The truth is, I never thought about Adam or any of the other leaders. I don't get wrapped up in other competitors' strategies or training. If you beat me on a given day, good for you. And that day, Adam had better tactics and deserved to win. Also, I have to give Lear credit. Adam was the best runner of a team Lear had followed all season. Of course he was going to put Adam in the starring role. By my final collegiate cross country race, Lear was right: my competition knew I wanted them to chase me. For the second time in 1998, Adam did just that. And thanks to Lear, I got to play a part in one of the most-loved running books ever. It is still one of my favorite races, and my hat is off to both of them.

𝒳 𝒳 𝒳

I was the 1998 Pac-10 cross country athlete of the year and won another conference track title in the 5000m the next spring. At the 1999 NCAA Championships in Boise, Idaho, Kip won the 5000 and I was ninth. In the 10,000, I placed sixth again, one spot ahead of Notre Dame's Ryan Shay. I wouldn't change any of my college career, my courses, my races, my training. All of it shaped who I am. But I certainly haven't forgotten that I'm one of the few guys who went pro from that period who never won a national collegiate championship in either track or cross country. I told Adam later that he cost me two titles—but I also told him I forgave him!

Coach Murray has said that he couldn't have asked for a better athlete than me. It wasn't just that I justified his investment of a full scholarship, he said. I was never angry, and if I was disappointed in a race, I didn't make a scene or blame it on anybody but myself. He said I was respected and liked by teammates and runners around the country. That makes me proud.

There was one exception to his praise. At the Mountain Pacific Regional indoor meet my senior year, I was anchoring the distance medley relay, the 1600-meter leg. Stanford was way ahead of us when I got the baton, but their runner miscounted the laps and started sprinting too early. When I passed him, I glared at him and kept staring as I went by, knowing he was exhausted and wouldn't challenge me. Coach Murray was not happy with me and let me know it. The truth is, I didn't think I'd ever beat that runner at a mile distance, and this was my best chance to do it. I got carried away in my excitement. But how Coach Murray responded had a big impact on me. He was serious but kind in letting me know that wasn't how sportsmen act. I've become known a little bit over the years for my celebrations, but I made sure never again to do so in a way that taunted another runner.

I wasn't sure I had a chance to become an elite runner, but three weeks after my collegiate career ended, I entered the USA Outdoor Track and Field Championships. Since I had qualified for the 10,000m, I figured why not. But I had no idea what to expect. Meb had recently become naturalized, and he and all the other best runners who were U.S. citizens would be there. Why shouldn't I join them?

3

REPRESENTING AMERICA . . . SECOND TIME'S A CHARM

Have you ever been to Seville, Spain? Neither have I.

I had plans to be there in August 1999, but I didn't get to go—and I had only myself to blame.

So much was happening to me so fast that year. I was finishing my second year of classes at the University of Arizona and my final year of collegiate eligibility on the track. On the heels of the NCAAs came the USA Outdoor Track and Field Championships at Hayward Field in Eugene, Oregon. I was running the 10,000m there in my first post-collegiate race. Though my fitness was still good, I had no idea what to expect in terms of my performance or how a big meet like this would be conducted.

Among those who would be competing—the very best professional distance runners in the country—I recognized plenty of names from the Pac-10 Conference. The top three in each event qualified for the IAAF World Track and Field Championships, which would be held in Seville. Representing the United States at the Worlds and the Olympics was the best opportunity for these guys to make their money. They weren't going to show me any mercy.

I felt strong and played it smart in my event. From the start, I and the rest of the field deferred to Alan Culpepper, the favorite. He took charge and we let him. But I hung close and managed to take third place in 28:28.26, six seconds behind Culpepper and four seconds behind runner-up Brad Hauser, one of the Stanford twins I had run against many times over the past two years. In an instant I had achieved something I didn't think possible—competing at a world-class competition as an American.

Soon, reality replaced my excitement. Paperwork, man. Take care of the details. That's my hard-earned advice. When you make a national team, the USA Track & Field officials spring into action. Seville was less than two months away even as we crossed the finish line. USATF makes sure you have everything in order so you can make the international trip—passport, visa, fingerprints, shots, a lot of stuff I had never given any thought to. When they said to send them my passport so they could process my application for the trip, I sent them the only document I had: my green card. I didn't think anything more about it until they called me a few days later and said, "Abdi, we need your passport." A green card shows you're in the United States legally, but it doesn't make you a citizen.

I hadn't been out of the United States since I arrived in 1993 through a program for Somali refugees. I'd been running and going to school for the past six years. My parents had always taken care of life's details. They gained citizenship while I was in college, so I assumed that meant I was a U.S. citizen too. What I discovered was that my two brothers and four sisters, all under age 18, received automatic citizenship when my parents did. But I was an adult by then; I had to apply on my own. The clock to Seville was ticking down, and time wasn't in my favor. I tried to fast-track citizenship, and there are mechanisms for doing that. But I couldn't get it done soon enough.

When Culpepper and Hauser were running around the track at Seville's *Estadio Olímpico*, I was watching it on TV in Tucson. While I was frustrated with myself and understood how I had made the mistake, I also felt like I had let down Meb Keflezighi, my UCLA friend who placed fourth at nationals and would have earned the third spot had I not been there. Meb didn't have a qualifying time that met the standard required to go to Worlds. By the time I got this all sorted out, he didn't have time to run a race that might have gotten him a qualifying mark. I'm a laid-back guy and don't mind making fun of myself. I let things go pretty quickly . . . grudges, regrets, mistakes. But more than 20 years later, this is still a little embarrassing because it wasn't fair to Meb.

Surely I'm the only athlete who has missed being on a national team because he didn't know he wasn't a citizen. Since then, I've been proud to represent the United States at the Olympics and the World Championships in track and cross country 13 times. But I can't count this one.

If anything, this incident reminds me how naïve I was back then. I didn't have big ambitions of being a runner; I had no big plans at all. Not getting the opportunity to be on the track in Seville in 1999 was an eye-opener. It made me realize I needed to take care of the details if I wanted to run at this level. The Olympic Trials were less than a year away, and I *really* wanted to wear a USA jersey. I barely remembered Somalia, but in America I had found a place where I could feel at home.

It was time to make it official.

$$\mathcal{F} \; \mathcal{F} \; \mathcal{F}$$

As it turns out, if you allow enough time, the process of becoming an American isn't so difficult. After passing the citizenship interview and exam, I was ready. I became a U.S. citizen on January 28, 2000, just under a month after I "officially" turned 23 years old. Like many refugees who arrive at a border without proof of birth, I was assigned a January 1 birthdate by immigration officials when I entered the United States.

In just a few weeks, I would compete for a spot on the U.S. team that would go to the IAAF World Cross Country Championships. My family had moved to Seattle, Washington, while I was in college, so Coach Murray joined me for a simple naturalization ceremony at the Pima County Courthouse in Tucson.

When you become naturalized as an American citizen, you stand in a strange sort of limbo. You are asked to support and defend the U.S. Constitution and the laws of the United States against its enemies. You give up allegiance to any other nation. I had no problem committing to that and taking the oath of allegiance. Also on that day, the emcee names each of the former countries of the new citizens. When I heard "Somalia," I stood up to acknowledge that was my old country. It's a funny place to stand. I felt like I had been practicing becoming an American for the past six-plus years. Because of my incredibly rewarding college experience—which was still happening, since I was taking a few more classes to complete my degree—I was comfortable saying I wanted to be a permanent part of American society. I felt American.

It was humbling and thrilling—I could feel a transition happening in real time. But as with my early days at U of A, where I felt increasingly accepted and open to all that was going on around me, it didn't change how I saw others. I didn't feel better than non–U.S. citizens I knew, just like I didn't feel better than other students at Arizona. I didn't feel like I was turning my back on Somalia, either. I was just stepping into who I wanted to be: an American. Likewise, I didn't feel better about myself when I beat other guys in races during my college career, and I didn't feel worse about myself when I lost to them. In all these situations, if you compare yourself to others and try to take on their journeys, you lose sight of where you want to go.

$$\mathcal{F} \; \mathcal{F} \; \mathcal{F}$$

One bit of good news that came out of my third-place finish at the 1999 USA Outdoors is that it caught the attention of Nike. People told me in college that I should get an agent and turn pro, but there are a lot of runners competing to get contracts. Just because you hear your friends and coaches saying that could happen doesn't mean it actually will. Not until Fred Harvey, who was the sprint coach at U of A, connected me with his former college teammate, John Capriotti, did professional running become a reality for me. Capriotti was already well known in the sport as Nike's director of global sports marketing, but I didn't know that. I was just happy he had faith in me. By late 1999, thanks to Nike, I had a career path.

My first international competition as a Nike-sponsored athlete was the 2000 World Cross Country Championships. After qualifying with a top-six finish at the USA National Cross Country Championships in Greensboro, North Carolina—and presenting my new, valid passport to the USATF officials—I was off to Vilamoura, Portugal, in March to compete as a member of Team USA. My citizenship was no longer in limbo, and Seville was a distant memory. I was going to the Iberian Peninsula after all; it just happened to be 130 miles farther west.

I placed 45th out of 160 overall finishers and was the second runner on a U.S. team that finished 11th out of 26 teams. (Meb was 26th; Brad Hauser was the third U.S. runner, in 58th place). The diversity of athletes made an impression on me. Sure, there had been lots of African Americans at college meets. Even in the Pac-10, I'd found African-born runners to connect with. Not surprisingly, that's exactly who I found at the World Cross Country Championships. There were stellar teams from Kenya, Ethiopia, Tanzania, Uganda, and Morocco, as well as African runners who were competing for Qatar, Bahrain, and other countries.

CHASING ABDI

"I'll never forget the first race I watched Abdi run. I was in high school at the time and Abdi was duking it out with Meb in a 10,000 race on the track. I can't remember who won that race but I do remember the fire I saw in the eyes of Abdi. Five years later I found myself walking the streets of Europe with Abdi as we were both under the same agent and traveling to various track meets to compete. I learned on that trip that the fire in Abdi's eyes is always burning bright when he is competing, but off the track and roads he is one of the most fun people to be around that I have ever come across. Abdi laughs easy, makes others laugh even easier, and is always seeing the bright side of life."

—Ryan Hall, American record holder in half marathon, two-time Olympian

When my family arrived in Tucson in 1993, we only knew one other family from Somalia, so Portugal became one of my first opportunities to meet other Somali-born people. Two stood out. One was Mohamed Suleiman, a Qatari who had won a bronze medal in the 1500m at the 1992 Barcelona Olympics. He was born in Somaliland, the separatist northern province where I also was born. I also met for the first time a 16-year-old who had been born in Somaliland and later moved to Mogadishu, just like my family, and eventually fled to the United Kingdom. Mohamed was 30 years old and nearing the end of his career, but the young Brit who took 25th place in the junior race was just starting his. I would have a lot more opportunities to talk to Mo Farah in the years to come.

I hit it off with most of the African-born runners I met. Even though we trained on different continents, when we saw each other at competitions it was easy to strike up conversations with them, whether in English, Swahili (for runners from countries like Kenya and Tanzania), or Somali. It became one of my favorite parts of making national teams—getting to travel and meet people from all over the world, including places I had been to but no longer remembered very well.

$$\t{5}\ \t{5}\ \t{5}$$

My showing in Portugal boosted my confidence heading into the U.S. Olympic Track and Field Trials. I was in good position to make the team in the 10,000m. Bob Kennedy and Culpepper would be formidable competition, but many U.S. runners had not met the Olympic qualifying standard as I had, including Meb. That meant I may be able to get a spot on the Olympic team even without a top-three finish.

It sounds crazy for me to say it now, but maybe I was a little overconfident when I arrived in Sacramento, California, for the U.S. Trials. I never take competition for granted. I respect the work all my competitors put in to get to that point. Also, I know how I feel when I line up for any race, and I suspect most of them feel the same way. I believe that I can win it, and if I didn't believe that was possible then I wouldn't bother being there. Still, I had now qualified for two national teams. Maybe success had come a little too quickly.

That might explain why I chose to wear a new pair of Jasari Zoom spikes that Nike gave me on July 14, 2000, the day of the 10,000-meter final at Hornet Stadium. I wore Jasari Zooms during races all the time anyway, so I figured it wouldn't hurt to just wear new ones. Besides, I knew they would look cool under the stadium lights, like a pair of Guccis rotating on a Fifth Avenue window display. Any runner knows you don't make dramatic changes to your gear on race day. Above all, you don't wear shoes that have never been worn before. Heck, I've been preaching simplicity in routine, training, diet . . . you name it . . . for years. But I didn't heed my own advice on that sticky summer night, and I was paying the price. After weaving my way through 34 guys to take the early lead, I soon began to struggle. I was doing everything I could to stay close to the leaders, but midway through the race, all I could focus on were my calves, piercing with pain. On the 17th lap of a 24-lap race, I was chewing on my jersey and seriously considering dropping out.

Coach Murray was watching from the west end of the stadium. He knew I was new to running races at this level and was in trouble. "Every time Abdi has had a bad race, he has started chewing on his jersey," he later told Greg Hansen of Tucson's *Arizona Daily Star* newspaper. "It had me very worried."

I was slowing down, but I calculated the situation and couldn't bear the thought of waiting four more years to make the Olympics. Meb had taken the lead at the three-mile mark and put a good distance between himself and Culpepper, who was still considered the favorite. (Kennedy was unable to run because he had not yet recovered from a bruised spine he received in a May automobile accident.) I had no delusions of catching the top two, but this was the Trials. A podium appearance would suffice, and no one around me seemed to be feeling much better in the California heat. I considered myself the leader in the race for third, and I determined I could handle another eight minutes worth of pain if it meant winning that self-concocted race—I also stopped sucking on my shirt.

"He told me he was scared," Coach Murray told Hansen later that night. "But he hung in there."

Yes, I did. I couldn't have written the rest of the race any better. I churned on, gaining confidence as I began lapping runners late in the race. I managed to forget the pain in my calves enough to open a gap between me and fourth place. Meb held off a furious late sprint by Culpepper to beat him by three-hundredths of a second, achieving his Olympic qualifying standard in the process. I came across 16 seconds later in 28:19.08. Shawn Found was fourth in 28:33.73. The next four runners, including fifth-place Brad Hauser (three Pac-10 guys in the top five!), came in over the next 15 seconds.

Culpepper and I congratulated each other at the finish. Meb was soaking up his victory around the near turn, slapping hands with the front row of his supporters, and I worked my way toward him, anxious to congratulate him. When he saw me, he put his hand out for a quick tap. "We did it!" I told him, but we were tired and it didn't register with him. He turned away, then turned back and put three fingers in the air. "You took third?" he seemed to say. I nodded, we hugged, and we jogged together toward the backstretch, blowing kisses to the 20,000 spectators as someone threw USA caps down to us.

I soon found Coach Murray, who hasn't gone to many of my races since I left college, in part because he gets so nervous for me. He congratulated me and then said, "What the hell happened? You didn't look right. You didn't look like yourself."

"My feet were killing me," I said.

Coach looked down and saw my brand-new spikes. "Where did you get those shoes? Those aren't the shoes you were supposed to be wearing."

I took off my shoes, and my feet were rubbed raw and bleeding. He rolled his eyes. Then we both laughed about it. Truthfully, I still wear brand-new racing flats for road races even though it's considered bad practice for runners to wear never-worn shoes in competition. I like having the extra cushion. And I wore Jasari Zooms for many more years on the track. But I'll admit it probably wasn't the best idea to do my first test run for a new pair of spikes in an Olympic qualifier.

"Just when I was about to drop out, I told myself that it would be four years until the next Olympic Trials," I told Hansen that night. "That's just too long. I told myself to bear down."

I chose exactly those words to tell Tucson readers what I had done: bear down.

Any U of A student knows those words well. It's been the school's official motto for nearly 100 years. The quarterback of the 1926 team, John B. Salmon, was in a car accident and suffered a severe spinal cord injury, dying a few weeks later. The coach, Pop McKale, told the team Salmon's last words to him were, "Tell them, tell the team to bear down," just before the Wildcats went out and defeated New Mexico State on the road, 7–0.

Movie-worthy words, for sure, and I took them to heart in Sacramento. By bearing down, I set in motion momentum that I feel I'm still riding. Maybe I make the 2004 Olympic team four years later, but maybe not. I seized the moment when sucking on my jersey and just finishing the race and planning to fight another day would have been easy to do. I was truly proud of myself. I'd been running for just over four years, and now I was headed to Sydney.

$$\tilde{\jmath}\ \tilde{\jmath}\ \tilde{\jmath}$$

A year earlier, I was a Somali working on a bachelor's degree, with no clear view of my future. Now I was an American professional runner with a shoe contract and an agent, the legendary Ray Flynn, who ran 89 sub-four-minute miles and competed in two Olympics for Ireland but is also well known for representing some of the biggest names in running over the past 30 years. I was believing in what was possible for me—what my coaches, family, and friends had been telling me in Tucson since my junior year. I no longer felt like a newcomer to the running world. I knew the pecking order in each event and was even beginning to learn some of the history of the sport, which I'd never paid much attention to before. After Billy Mills, the namesake of the hill where I battled Goucher at the final mile of the 1998 NCAA cross country meet, congratulated me in

Sacramento, it even dawned on me that I might someday become part of that history.

It's easy to feel scattered when your life is moving like a blur. I tell myself in those moments to stay grounded and remind myself of what I really want.

The next morning, I made sure to be the first in line to fill out all the documents needed to attend the 2000 Olympics. No oversights, no mistakes allowed this time. I missed Seville; I wasn't missing Sydney. Nike set up a news conference for me near the Sacramento State University campus that morning.

I was asked if it might have been easier to run for Somalia.

"No," I said, "because I never ran in Somalia. I have only run in America, and now I'm an American. This is my country."

First Olympic Ring

Sydney

E ven if it hadn't been my first Olympics, Sydney would have been a spectacle to remember. The Australians were amazing hosts and the city was clean, inviting, and up to the task of ringing in the 21st century. (Yeah, technically the millennium would not end until New Year's Eve leading into 2001, but for me at least, Sydney felt like a fitting welcome to new possibilities in my life that a new century—and new citizenship—symbolize).

It is one of the few events in the world where you can have that much human diversity all in one place for two weeks. Just me and my U of A friends made for an international forum: Ryk Neethling, one of South Africa's star swimmers; Patrick Nduwimana, my 800-meter Wildcat teammate, who introduced me briefly to the other five members of his Burundi track squad—four men running distance events and a 15-year-old named Diane Nukuri, who was running the 5000m and carrying the flag for her country at the Opening Ceremonies.

Coach Murray prepared me so well for the 2000 Olympics, but I did defy him when he told me not to walk in the Opening Ceremonies. He said it saps your energy, but I couldn't avoid a big party like that. He understood, but he wasn't happy about it.

I knew a medal was a long shot, but, hey, if I line up on a given day, I believe I'm in as good a place as everybody else there. Back then, there was a preliminary round to cull down the field to 20. I set a personal best, 28:09.04, to advance to the finals three nights later. In the finals, 13 of us broke loose by the 3000-meter mark and sustained our positions for another mile or so. With 12 laps to go, I felt strong. Since I like being chased, I decided to surge. I was leading the Olympic 10,000m and even opened up a gap of about 10 meters. But it was short-lived. After another 500 meters, first Paul Tergat of Kenya and then Haile Gebrselassie of Ethiopia—two legends—reeled me in. But with less than 11 laps to go, I remained in the long, fast-accelerating line of 13 runners.

I'm convinced I could have finished in the top five if I'd known what the heck I was doing. The final lap had Tergat in front but the favorite, Gebrselassie, staying close, along with three others. As the crowd roared, I found myself watching their mad dash to the finish—with Gebrselassie overtaking Tergat in the final 50 meters—on the giant Jumbotron screen above the stadium. I became a fan when I should have been bearing down! I got passed by Toshinari Takaoka of Japan, Karl Keska of Great Britain, and Aloys Nizigama of Burundi on the homestretch.

On the plus side, I set my second PR in a week with a time of 27:46.17 and finished 10th. Meb was two places and seven seconds behind me. American distance running had been in a long period of decline on the international stage at the end of the 20th century, but the United States track and field establishment was determined to do something about that. After my whirlwind year, I now felt confident that I could contribute to a new era.

Part II
Athens 2004

A LESSON
IN BELONGING

———

"Abdi's always attentive. I'm amazed at what he's done.
You've gotta hand it to him. He did the hard work.
It wasn't organized hard work, but maybe that's the key to it.
More than anybody I know, he's done it on his own. He wanted
to seek excellence in running. That was his big motivation.
He's developed into a wonderful person and one of America's
greatest runners. I'd put him on par with Hall, Shorter, Meb."

—Coach Joe Vigil, my friend and driver
to my first altitude-training camp

4

WE HAVE
A SECOND BREATH

My 2001 season began where my 2000 season had left off—full of promise.

I qualified for the World Cross Country Championships in Oost-ende, Belgium, which was held on a March day better suited for ducks than humans. Those were the worst conditions of any race I've ever run, other than maybe the frigid 2018 Boston Marathon. At least the cross country meet was over after 12K. The wind was whipping off the Atlantic coast, and several times I expected my Nikes to get sucked underground and lost forever in the sloppiest mud pools. Fortunately, I had the foresight to tie my shoelaces tight and tape them down.

Tactically, I ran a good race. I knew I needed to go as hard as I could from the start, then hold my position. It was going to be next to impossible to pass people late on the 2K loop course at the Hippodrome Wellington.

In a sign of how the U.S. distance-running program was regaining a spark after a long dormant period, we took the bronze medal as a team with 87 points—behind the incomparable Kenyans' 16th consecutive victory and the runner-up French—the first U.S. podium since 1986. Only 11 seconds separated Bob Kennedy (12th overall in 40:43; Meb, 13th in 40:46; and me, 15th in 40:54). The rest of the squad—Nick Rogers, Greg Jimmerson, and Matt Downin—all finished in the top half of the field.

At that time, there really weren't professional teams in the United States. We all trained in different places, so this event was one of the few places that felt like being on a college squad again. My training group then consisted of occasional workouts with the University of Arizona team. The World Cross Country Championships is one of my favorite events—the best 1500m, 5K, 10K, and marathon runners in the world all thrown together for 12 kilometers on a unique course in unknown conditions. How much better does running get than that?

☞ ☞ ☞

In June, I won the national 10,000m title at the USA Track and Field Championships in Eugene. Coupled with strong showings in 5000m and 10,000m races throughout the spring and summer, I had high hopes of landing a top-five finish at my first World Track and Field Championships in early August. Instead, I finished 19th in the 10,000m in 28:34.38 and was never in contention. I didn't watch the video screen in Edmonton, Canada, like I did in Sydney, but I might as well have. Better yet, I should have stayed home and received my bachelor's degree in person. Though my athletic eligibility ended in 1999, I still had a few courses to take to complete my retail and consumer studies program. I finished the last of them in summer 2001, just before leaving for Edmonton. Diplomas were handed out the day after the Worlds, but I got mine once I returned to Tucson. I remember walking across campus in nearly 120-degree heat to pick it up at my academic advisor's office. No big commencement ceremony, but that was fine. My family was in Seattle, and I was traveling the world in my career. I would surely find a way to use my degree later.

☞ ☞ ☞

I wanted to put the World Championships race behind me, and I did that with a fifth-place showing (28:08.02) in the 10,000m at the Goodwill Games in Brisbane, Australia. That was on September 7. I had barely gotten back home when my concerns about mile splits and race results became much less important to me. I was in my Tucson living room on Tuesday morning, September 11, when a friend called and asked if I was watching TV. I tuned in along with my fellow U.S. citizens and the world to discover that terrorists had flown two planes into the Twin Towers of the World Trade Center.

I had been a U.S. citizen for just a year and a half and had experienced so many good things in this country. But that was a sad day for everyone. It was an attack on America, but even more so than terrorist acts that occur at embassies, in the air, and sadly all too often in other public places around the world, this felt like a violation of free society itself. America had that symbolic value to people who cared about such things—and as someone who felt deeply fortunate to have received an opportunity here, I certainly did. During the chaos and fear of a time like that, you hold on to the values and people that are important to you. That sustained me.

As a Muslim man with a name like Abdihakim Abdirahman, I expected to hear some pretty awful things that autumn after 9/11. Since I traveled a lot, I thought I might get questioned at airports. I was even prepared for it. I only ran one more race before the season ended—a second-place finish at the Mobile 10K in Alabama in early November. I'm happy to say that I did not experience direct discrimination in the months and years following that tragedy. Like friends of mine, I was fearful and looked at my surroundings differently, but running had taught me it was best to stay in a positive frame of mind and not focus on things I couldn't control. I surrounded myself with people who wanted all of us to get along. From my parents' actions when Somalia was falling into civil war and during the uncertainty of a Kenyan refugee camp, they taught me those lessons whether they knew it or not.

I thought of my parents a lot during these weeks when people seemed unsure who to trust. My parents had been living a good life in Somalia until they had to start over. My father, Mohammed, had gone to the Soviet Union for university and worked as an administrator in the United Kingdom. I even remembered seeing a photo of him standing off the Russian cold in a bushy coat. My parents moved from Hargeisa in Somaliland to Mogadishu in 1971. My father got a job with Conoco, and my mother,

Halima, was a secretary at the Press and Translation Office for the federal government. Her job was to type up the translations she was given of English newspapers so that President Mohamed Siad Barre could read them in Somali. This was before he turned on his citizens. My mother would sometimes take the transcriptions to him herself. Personally, he was nice to her, and for a while she saw him doing positive things for Somalia.

Siad Barre had come to power in 1969 in a military coup. He tried to unify the many clans and cultures of Somalia, which had only been an independent country since 1960, in a socialist state. Initially, that was popular. The economy and military were strong. He had the Somali language developed into a standard national writing system for the first time and encouraged people to eat seafood from the Indian Ocean so they wouldn't be so reliant on livestock. He developed a nationwide tree-planting campaign to prevent erosion and improve agricultural capabilities. But as the years went on, he chose to punish clans who weren't his. And he got greedy.

Siad Barre tried to create a Greater Somalia by bringing in ethnic Somalis who lived in other countries in the Horn of Africa . . . Kenya, Djibouti, and Ethiopia. Soon after I was born, in 1977, he invaded the Ogaden region of Ethiopia. When the Soviet Union turned on him and supported Ethiopia, he became an outcast to other Communist countries and sought support from the United States and the western world. His retreat meant he lost trust among his citizens. Life in Somalia gradually began to descend into chaos in the 1980s. My mother, seeing how his loyalty to his clan was influencing Siad Barre's decisions for the country, had requested transfers from him and his staff before. During the uncertainty of the Ogaden war, she was able to change jobs to a nationalized sugar cane factory.

My family is Isaaq, a clan located in Somaliland in the far north of the country. I was born in Hargeisa, the capital of Somaliland, because my mother wanted to give birth to her first child where her extended family could provide support. We went back to Mogadishu soon after I came into the world. My parents adapted to the new normal of caring for a baby. They both had decent jobs, and our family grew as my brothers, Ayanle (1981) and Salaad (1984), and sisters, Hoda (1985) and Hibo

(1988), joined us. Nationwide, though, Siad Barre remained in power, and my parents along with many others saw that he was becoming paranoid.

Increasingly he began killing political opponents and anyone he thought was disloyal to him. Because Somaliland has long been contested, it was one of the earliest hot spots of the Somali civil war. Starting in 1987, Siad Barre committed genocide against the Isaaq there in what was called the "Hargeisa holocaust," killing perhaps hundreds of thousands of people. Anyone who had lived for any period of time in Hargeisa, my parents included, knew friends and family who disappeared or were killed. My home city was destroyed from the fighting and became known as the "Dresden of Africa."

While Mogadishu, where we were living, is a nearly 900-mile drive from Hargeisa, my parents saw how dangerous life might get for us. By January 1991, the war between several rebel groups and Siad Barre's military continued. With smoke literally visible in Mogadishu and my mother five months pregnant, they made the hard decision. Taking a jug of milk, a jug of water, and five kids, they locked the door to our house at dawn and started walking west to Afgooye, a town 17 miles away, where a friend of my dad's lived. Many people were fleeing on foot and by car to get away from the war. We arrived in Afgooye after dark, and the family gave us food and rugs and blankets so we could sleep outside on their land. As hungry as we were, we just wanted to rest. We were exhausted but hopeful that we could stay for a few weeks until order was restored and it was safe to return to our house.

Within a few days, it was clear to my parents that was wishful thinking. We weren't going back home anytime soon. Siad Barre fled the country, leaving a power vacuum in which all sides would be emboldened to do whatever it took to seize control. There were three main rebel groups and loyalists in Siad Barre's military—each with its own grudges and agendas—trying to establish their strength in whatever sections of Somalia they could. More and more people fled west from the capital as we had done. We stayed put for a couple weeks in Afgooye, an area surrounded by lots of agriculture—sugar cane, corn, bananas. That lushness meant lots of mosquitoes, and my mother and I both contracted malaria.

My parents decided we should go to Kismayo, a coastal city 300 miles south, where my father had family. There, we could also get better medical care. I recovered from malaria sickness quickly with medication. But because my mother was midway through her pregnancy, she couldn't take the drugs. For a month, we stayed in Kismayo. My mother recovered, but the situation in Mogadishu and all over the country continued to worsen. Outside of Kismayo, United Somali Congress rebels were trying to dislodge soldiers still fighting for Siad Barre.

My parents, along with thousands of others, had to make another tough decision. With no certainty that Somalia would stabilize anytime soon, they chose to get out. We were among the first of the massive wave of refugees leaving the country in early 1991. We had hoped to get to Malindi, in Kenya, on a 60-foot *dhow* trading boat, but word spread that people were paying fares up to $500. Even at that outrageous price, it was soon full. The boat was built for 150 people, but twice that number were on board when it left Kismayo. Meanwhile, my family was still searching for another solution. Two or three boats a day were leaving from Kismayo, but most didn't carry many passengers. That *dhow* had seemed like our best hope for a fast exit. A man heard my parents talking with other refugees about what to do. He said he had a small boat leaving the next day and he could take all seven of us. In Kismayo, we were not far from the Kenyan border, but Malindi was still 250 miles of travel on the Indian Ocean. We got on board and left Somalia. Our locked house in Mogadishu was only getting farther away with each southward mile. There was no turning back now.

As we neared our destination, Malindi dispatchers directed our captain to another dock. Soon, we saw evidence of the reason why. Bodies and debris from the boat we had wanted to be on were floating in the water. We found out later that in addition to the 300 people who had boarded the *dhow* at Kismayo, 400 more were picked up at the Kenyan island of Lamu. More than 150 died as the overcrowded boat hit a coral reef six miles from shore. Many who didn't make it were trapped in the lower deck, trampled or trapped under a plastic tarp. Mothers held their dead children closely in their arms.

Some 500 survivors were bused farther down the coast to Mombasa, where a refugee camp was being constructed. But seeing all the death and destruction had taken its toll on my mother. As she told me later, "That's when I realized, 'I'm out of my country and I do not know where I'm heading.' We had no sense of direction or what next. A question mark was on top of our heads all the time." The stress and perhaps the seasickness exhausted my mother, who was only six months into her pregnancy. The Italian woman Giannina was among the locals helping the new arrivals, and when she heard my parents asking for help, she got my mother to the Aga Khan hospital immediately. My sister was born soon after they arrived, weighing not much more than a pound. Her eyes barely opened; even her ears weren't fully developed. But our "miracle child," as my mother called her, was alive. All of us were alive.

𝒵 𝒵 𝒵

We kids trusted our parents and did what we were told on our journey from Mogadishu to Afgooye to Kismayo and then out of Somalia to Malindi. They seemed so sure about each step they took; I had no idea until I was much older how scared they were. They hid their fear because they didn't want us to feel the same way.

I don't remember the details of that period very well anymore, and it's not something my family has talked much about over the years. "It was an awful period of our life," my mother says. "We had no home, nothing with us. We just lived day by day. We didn't know when we would get food the next morning, but somehow it just came through the hands of Allah. It's painful to go back to that. A lot of people, it didn't work out for them."

Thank God it wasn't our time to go. My family was still intact. Now, as I was building my professional running career a decade later, my family was all in the United States and even bigger: a fourth sister, Hamdi, had been born in Tucson in 1996. Though my family moved to Seattle while I was at University of Arizona, we remained in regular contact. If it wasn't exactly the American dream, I was grateful my parents had the resources and resolve to take care of their young family and we had the good fortune to make a new life here. The United States can seem removed from the fighting going on around the world, but nowhere is entirely safe. I found myself craving stability after 9/11. With loving family and friends and the good fortune to have a job that allowed me to release my emotions and energy with hard physical workouts, I found calm during a difficult time.

I thought a lot about friends like Meb and Kip during the months after the attacks, and had plenty of conversations with Kip before and after our training sessions when he moved to Tucson in 2002. We came from three different African countries, but we had each been given incredible opportunities in our adopted country.

Kip grew up in almost a middle-class existence in the North Rift of western Kenya. His older sister, Mary Chepkemboi, was an African champion runner who inspired him to see the possibilities. Not only that, his parents were supportive of a girl running, which was rare at the time. They encouraged him and his six sisters and three brothers to participate in the sport. But he saw poverty all around him, and he knew how difficult life could be in his home country. He told me that his sister gained a sense of freedom through running that was difficult for girls to experience then, and he feels that I did the same in my life when I discovered the sport later.

Meb escaped Eritrea, which was still fighting for independence from Ethiopia, with his family when he was 12 years old, about the same time my family left Somalia. His father was a vocal supporter of independence and had to flee to Italy and send money back to his family. Meb also spoke no English and had never considered running when his family settled in San Diego with few resources.

My two friends and I didn't talk in a whole lot of detail about our childhoods, but we knew we had been given a gift by arriving on these shores and discovering that we had a talent for running. Meb and I roomed together in 2000 at the Olympic Village in Sydney and also at the 2001 World Cross Country Championships. I spent a lot of time with Kip in Sydney too. They were role models for me when I was still brand new to the sport, and I tried to listen to them like they were my big brothers. They've been role models for millions of others since, as their stellar

CHASING ABDI

Excerpt from "Brief Chat: Abdirahman and Lagat," an article by Peter Gambaccini in *Runner's World,* April 4, 2012.

Peter: What do you each think is the number one thing you've learned from the other?

Me: One thing I'll never take for granted is discipline and goal setting and hard work, and that's the discipline—take running as your job and as your profession. That's one thing I learned from Bernard, and I'm so thankful for you teaching me that, Bernard. I know a lot of people that know me before, first couple years I was a pro runner, I enjoyed life, I did a lot of stuff, and there's no regret there, and that's what life is all about. You learn from it. But there's a point in your life when you learn, and I just happen to have one of my great friends who happens to be one of the greatest runners of all time who is teaching me the ropes basically, and I took from him.

Bernard Lagat: One thing about Abdi that I really admire a lot is his ability to do extra hard work when it's needed. He always has time for his training and time just to relax and be himself. So that's the thing that defines the strong athlete. What I like about Abdi is also the ability and that virtue of [being] willing to listen. It doesn't matter what you tell him, he's going to listen and he never gives up . . . Bounce back whenever you have an obstacle. He may have been having a few injuries, but he doesn't give up. That is something I always remember very clearly, even whenever I have my small problem, I think of a bigger problem that Abdi has had and you overcame it, and I always think, this is how I want to achieve what I have to do, because Abdi has done it, and I always see this as an example.

careers have unfolded. Years after 9/11, when a journalist asked whether Meb and I were living the American dream, I told him that our experiences as immigrants motivate us. "We know where we came from in life," I said. "We have a second breath. We talk about what we have accomplished, and we are grateful for the opportunity we have. We never take it for granted."

That is still true. I tease Meb now that he may have victories from the New York City and Boston marathons and an Olympic medal, but while he's sitting around in retirement, I'm beating the young guys. Kip is one of my best friends, and I still see him regularly in Tucson. I have all the respect in the world for both of them. They are not just incredible American runners and international ambassadors for the sport, they have been patient with me. They've seen me when I'm down and they've seen me at my happiest. No matter where your friends come from, you can't ask for more than that.

5

SEEKING BALANCE
AT HOME AND ABROAD

After 9/11, the world underwent a shift. Anyone who was alive at the time understood that. The West was learning fast about the Muslim world, and there was a sense of fear and prejudice coming from many directions.

The United States was contemplating invasion of Iraq, hardline security measures were put in place in major cities all over the globe, and faithful, law-abiding Muslims felt like they were being lumped in with radicals who had a violent, misguided interpretation of Islam. I've seen what extremists all over the world can do in politics and religion. No matter how they dress up what they say to justify their violent talk and actions, extremists divide us for their own benefit. When they succeed, it chips away at our common humanity.

I've always had friends from all different faiths and political leanings. I like hearing about people's stories and sharing mine, but I never want to judge them by ideology or theology. I certainly don't try to convert others to my religion or let others feel they need to change my beliefs. I judge people by how they treat me and others; if I don't believe they are a positive influence, then I don't hang around them.

That approach to people helped me see the world differently than how news reports depicted the world at that time. I was traveling all over the globe as a new American citizen in the early 2000s. I recognize that I was insulated from some of the hate that others who look like me or have a name like mine experienced because I was a competitive athlete—an invited guest—when I came to a city. Still, I looked for the good in people, and let me tell you, when you're looking for something, you're more likely to find it. Even in high-stress times, there's a lot of good out there.

I make it a point to talk with people even when I'm not feeling social. One time, my flight arrived very late and I took a cab to my hotel. My race was two days away. I just wanted to get to bed and then shake off jet lag the next morning. The cab driver, recognizing I looked like a runner, started talking to me. He asked where I was from and how good I was and overall just seemed sincerely interested in learning about me. I was exhausted, but I realized it was important to keep the conversation going. Maybe it mattered to him because he wanted to learn about my experience or just to tell his kids he spoke to a professional athlete. Who knows? That wasn't the point. My job, I determined, was to answer his questions and help him understand something new.

Maybe it was important to me too—an opportunity to learn how we all want to feel like we belong to something bigger than ourselves and build positive relationships. I do my best to not act like an entitled athlete, but this mindset goes well beyond sports. We all have a responsibility to find common ground.

Sports can be a means to do just that. We all know the Olympics captures the attention of the whole world in a way no other sporting event does—with the possible exception of the World Cup in soccer. But World Championships are just as competitive and prestigious as the Olympics to the professionals inside the sport. From 2000 to 2008, I represented the United States on national teams at either the World Outdoor Track and Field Championships, World Cross Country Championships, or Olympics every year except 2006, and that year I set my marathon personal best. I won national titles on the track and the roads in distances ranging from the 10K to the half marathon.

What stands out in my mind even more from this period, though, is how much I enjoyed meeting people from all parts of the world. I listened to locals tell me about the history all around us in places like Dublin, Rome, and Brussels. Full stadiums and hippodromes cheered us on around Europe, no matter which countries we represented. I raced against some of the best runners who have ever competed, including Ethiopia's legendary Kenenisa Bekele. That guy just seemed to float over cross country courses.

Back home in the United States, I was a pro athlete by summer 2001, but I still enjoyed enthusiastic college-town crowds when I returned to running hotbeds such as Des Moines, Eugene, Palo Alto, and Boulder.

I was experiencing the world's great scenery and cities with famous runners, decent people, and caring fans who knew the history of their cities and their meets, and the times of their favorite athletes. Those fans from all over cared about the sport and made me want to learn more and be a member of the running community.

Which is not to say I didn't enjoy my return to Tucson after every trip. I don't like making massive changes, and I stay loyal to what works. Life there is slow and simple for me, with plenty of training routes to choose from. People knew me in Tucson, not just from my university days but from having lived there for nearly a decade at that point. I was a respectable citizen in a hip desert town of half a million people. Who wouldn't want that?

CHASING ABDI

LetsRun.com has covered our sport thoroughly for years, but their writers also know how to have fun. They wrote a spoof article in 2003. The joke was that David Krummenacker and Kip Lagat were trash-talking each other before the upcoming 1500m race at the adidas Boston Games, and Kip eventually attacked David with a Gatorade bottle (photos were included!):

"Fortunately, the fight was stopped when Abdi Abdirahman, the Mayor of Tucson distance running himself, pulled up in his 2002 Yukon Denali with 22-inch wheels, incredible sound system, and DVD player inside. Lagat and Krummenacker quickly hugged each other and apologized and jumped into the back of Abdi's truck.

"'Everyone knows this is Abdi's town. He went to high school and college here and lives here now. David and I are nothing in this town. I didn't want to upset Abdi, and wanted to cruise the town with him, so I quit beating up on David,' said Lagat.

"Added Krummenacker, 'Abdi is the local hero. Everybody loves Abdi. It's kind of funny, we'll go out sometimes (without Abdi) and there will be a bunch of runners and someone will figure one of those guys must be Abdi and they'll just say, Hi Abdi.'"

I'm always happy to be cast in the role of peacemaker. Even if it was just made up this time, I think it's true most days.

The article had photos of me—"The Mayor himself," according to the caption—showing off my red Denali. I had bought it after I signed my first contract with Nike. I know shiny things don't bring happiness, but I loved that ride for years. It meant something to me. A few years earlier, I could never have imagined buying a car like that. Once I had the means, I decided to treat myself. I never regretted it.

At the very end of the article was this:

"*Editor's note:* If track and field was a bit more mainstream, maybe you'd see more articles like this one. But we made most of it up. (In real life, Lagat and Krummenacker often run together as on the day of this photo). However, the photos are legitimate, and the last quote by Krummenacker is a real quote. Seriously. We promise."

It's good to be home, where everybody knows your name . . . even if they don't always know exactly what you look like.

🏃 🏃 🏃

One of the more interesting jobs in distance running is being a "rabbit." These top-level runners serve as pacesetters for would-be record-breakers in distance races. It's not bad work if you can get it, sort of like a rodeo clown or a backup singer . . . a selfless job where you're on the stage doing important but often unrecognized work so the headliners—the bull rider, the lead singer, the record-seeking runner—can look good.

When I took my official recruiting visit to the University of Arizona, I stayed with Bob Keino, one of the best milers in the Pac-10 Conference at the time. His brother Martin had been an NCAA champion at the 1994 cross country meet and the 1995 outdoor 5000m race on the track. Their father, Kipchoge Keino of Kenya, is considered "the father of Kenyan distance running." He kick-started a half century of African distance-running greats with gold medals at the 1968 and 1972 Olympics, broke world records at 3000m and 5000m, and has been honored for humanitarian work for starting a foundation, a school, and an orphanage in Eldoret, Kenya. I knew none of this at the time.

Martin was living in Oregon then, beginning his career in sport marketing and design with Nike while still training to fulfill a daunting goal: the 1996 Kenyan Olympic team. He was one of the top 10 middle-distance runners in the world, but most of the others on that list were also Kenyans. He barely missed making the team, coming up one place short at the Kenyan Olympic Trials. As someone who has competed in six U.S. Olympic Trials races, I can tell you how stressful it is to consider the split-second difference between third and fourth in a do-or-die race.

For the next decade after he graduated from Arizona, Martin was one of track's most successful rabbits. It fit Martin's giving personality well. Once my pro career on the track began, I even competed in several races on the European Golden League circuit where Martin would take the lead for a few laps before peeling off.

It seems crazy to me now that I didn't know the Keino name then, but I realized that to me they represented how I could feel connected to the globe from my home base of Tucson. Bob transferred before I signed to run for Arizona, so I unfortunately never became his teammate, but the family is still an inspiration to me. Martin became a sought-after motivational speaker and is now CEO of Keino Sports Group Ltd. in Eldoret.

Mr. Keino has been quoted as saying, "I'm just a simple man with simple dreams that used my God-given talents to help make a difference and create a better future for our children.

"We come into this world with nothing . . . and depart this world with nothing . . . it's what we contribute to the community that is our legacy."

The Keinos were in an influential position in their community and made a difference. We all can do something. It may not be as big a project as setting up a global foundation and an orphanage like Kip Keino and his wife Phyllis did, but we should all do what we can to improve the world.

$$\tilde{\jmath} \quad \tilde{\jmath} \quad \tilde{\jmath}$$

Leading up to the 2004 Olympic Trials in Sacramento, California, Meb asked me numerous times to join him at Mammoth Lakes, California, where he and a small group of hand-picked men and women had been training as part of a project to rejuvenate American distance running. I'd had invitations at other times since the Mammoth team began back in 2001.

Sure, sounds good, I'll be there, I would say. And I always thought I would. But I always backed out before I traveled up there. When I got back from competition, I liked chilling at home in Tucson with my friends. I was still doing the work to be ready for big races, so I figured it wasn't worth going. It didn't dawn on me that they might be holding a room for me or anything like that.

When the Trials came around in July, Meb was friendly enough beforehand, as always. In the race itself, I figured we would both run together until the final lap and then go all out to see who would take the victory. I knew we both had excellent chances to make the team, and that seemed the best way to get it done. But whenever I tried to take the lead, Meb wouldn't let me. He ran away from me and everybody else in 27:36.49. I was second in 27:55.00, and Dan Browne was third in

28:07.47. Meb was too gracious to say it out loud, but it was as though he was saying to me, Where have you been? We could have been getting this good together.

Meb had already qualified for the Olympics in the marathon. In Athens a month later, he chose to compete in the longer event and nearly pulled off a gold medal. Meanwhile, I finished a disappointing 15th in the 10,000. I knew Meb's coach, Bob Larsen, from their UCLA days, and Coach Larsen was also the U.S. distance coach at the Olympics that year. Coach Murray had already said the Mammoth group would be beneficial for me, though he ultimately always left it up to me where I would train. Coach Larsen said the invitation still stood. He later told me that I would have fit in with their squad over the previous few years. I had a reputation for not being focused, but they also knew I would not back down from anybody in training and would be a good teammate.

Coach Murray has always expected me to make the final call on anything running-related. He tells me what he thinks about workouts, strategies, where I should be, and who I should train with, but then knows I'm the one who has to follow through; it's my life. Part of that trust was a reminder to me that I could be successful wherever I trained, and I ultimately decided after the 2000 Olympics to stay with what was working for me: Tucson, Coach Murray, familiarity. Coach only advised me to do what I felt comfortable with.

Even though I implicitly trusted him, he wisely knew that it needed to be my decision. I had asked him to keep working with me after the Sydney Games, even though he had his own collegiate program to direct. He graciously accepted, even refusing to take money for his work. I love the quote he gave Sarah Barker, a reporter for *Deadspin*, in 2016. She asked him about how runners want to hire Coach Murray based on the success he's had with me, but he always tells them no.

"Nah, I'm not interested in having other athletes," he said, "and besides, I'd feel like I had to charge them something. I've never taken a penny for coaching Abdi. I just enjoy being around him; it keeps me busy. He's always saying, 'Coach, let me pay you.' But you know, I'm just watching him run 25 laps of a track. I can't actually do anything. I don't feel like I need to take his money; he earned it. I just enjoy coaching him."

Is it any wonder I love the guy?

He pushed me hard, and as in college, I was hungry for any workout he gave me. Though he retired from a distinguished career at U of A in 2002, he continued to coach me, and I suspect he will until I retire. If he ever asks for back pay, I'm going to have one hell of a bill!

After Meb's and Deena Kastor's showings in Athens, a light bulb went off for me. Only about a dozen men and women were getting asked to go to Mammoth. It was a hot ticket, really ever since Meb ran a 27:13.98 American record in the 10,000 back in 2001. Once Meb took silver and Deena a bronze in the 2004 Olympic marathons, the desire to join that group only grew among elite distance runners. I learned later that Coach Larsen even turned down national champions because he knew the chemistry of the group was important in such a remote area with not much to do except run and hang out—and yet he wanted me there if I wanted to be there. Here I was, taking that opportunity for granted.

I felt like I had aged so much more than four years since the Sydney Games. Not in a bad way, necessarily, and don't get me wrong: I enjoyed myself. I was just 27 years old, after all! I had a reputation for liking to party, and I did soak up all I could from the cities I visited—the food and drink, the culture, the jokes, the ideas. I sought out fun, for sure. The more I interacted with others, the more I realized most people just want to get along peacefully. There are exceptions, of course, and you might consider this naïve. I see it as a gift, the opportunity to learn from others, and that gets me through difficult times. I can't help but think this approach would make the world a better place. Not everything has to be a battle for property or power or profit, or even a gold medal. Sometimes, eating lunch with another person or telling them an entertaining story is the most human thing to do.

On the track, I may not have yet been a student of the sport, but I was becoming more intuitive. I've never spent a lot of time with prerace strategy, choosing instead to push the pace when I can and read situations as they unfold during the race. Running to me is competition in its purest form. Sure, runners get caught up with their times and personal bests and course records—I can too. But at the end of the day, a race is a challenge at one moment in time to see who will rise to meet it. Each competitor has strengths and weaknesses; the key is finding out on the spot which are yours and theirs, then responding. It's a cat-and-mouse game, or perhaps another form of hide-and-seek. That's the most fun part of serious racing, not chasing best times. It was effective for me because I was increasingly confident and willing to learn something new each time out. I knew what to expect at races from myself and most of the competition, and I'd like to think I was earning the respect of the best American runners and many around the world.

Experiences like the Trials and Olympics in 2004 taught me I still had a lot of learning to do, though. In some ways I felt more mature—as an athlete and as a person. I was out of college and figuring out how I wanted to make a living, how I wanted to make my mark. In other ways, I didn't want to get too serious. Maybe that's the internal tension of everybody in their 20s. Maybe 9/11 magnified that whole process.

After Athens, my respect for Meb and Deena and what they and their coaches and other athletes were accomplishing in Mammoth made it easy to say yes. I had trained with Meb before big international meets and at the Olympic Training Center in Chula Vista, California, but never a dedicated altitude camp.

I had been doing a lot of training on my own, and to this day, I still enjoy my solo runs. But this was a thrilling opportunity to be part of a team every day again for a while, take advice from other experts all around me, perhaps even try a new event . . . the marathon.

It was the first time—but certainly not the last—that I found comfort in training partners working out in high places.

6

ACCEPTING A NEW TRAINING
GROUND IN MAMMOTH

The longest road trip I ever took was 722 miles over mountains, across deserts, and through deep valleys with a talkative 70-year-old man who wouldn't let me drive.

If that sounds like a disaster, I should be clear that it was actually one of the most enjoyable trips I've ever taken—another reminder of how much support I've received during my life.

American distance running was struggling at the start of the 21st century. The 2000 Sydney Olympics had resulted in a complete medals shutout for Americans in races longer than 1500m, a drought that had become the norm. In the marathon, only one man and one woman even made the qualifying standard. In seven Olympiads since 1972 (not including the 1980 Moscow Games, which were boycotted by the United States), only five American men and women reached the podium out of 171 Olympic medals awarded—less than 3 percent of the total. In 1999, for the first time in some six decades that *Track & Field News* magazine had been in existence, there was not a single U.S. man in the world's top 10 in the 800m, 1500m, 3000m steeplechase, 5000m, 10,000m, or marathon.

Team Running USA California was dreamed up in 2001 by USA Track & Field, the sport's national federation, and Running USA, a non-profit devoted to promoting U.S. distance running, to stem the tide. The plan was to mimic the African altitude camps that Kenyans and Moroccans had pioneered. The term "game-changer" gets thrown around a lot, but given the performances by American runners in the 21st century, I think it's appropriate here. By the time Meb and Deena broke through in Athens with medals, other American teams were cropping up: Nike's Oregon Project and the Bowerman Track Club. Brooks began sponsoring the Hansons Distance Project. All of these were examples of the benefits of camaraderie and shared resources that pro running teams enjoyed.

The competition raised everybody's expectations. A lot of runners were meeting the Olympic standard. Making the American team was becoming more difficult, which in turn was a lot of fun. No longer was just showing up at international meets something to be celebrated; we all wanted to reach higher goals, including perhaps some medals for ourselves.

After I returned from Athens, I didn't need convincing to go to my first altitude-training camp. Endurance athletes have understood for decades now that training at high altitude, if done properly, can potentially benefit their performance. The science behind altitude training, in short, is that when oxygen is thinner, the body will adapt by increasing its production of red blood cells and hemoglobin, which will then allow for better cardiovascular output for a time back at lower elevations.

Beyond the short-term physiological benefits, there was also the possibility that other rewards of being part of Team Running USA California might be longer lasting.

☞ ☞ ☞

My chauffeur to Mammoth Lakes also happened to be one of the sport's living legends: Coach Joe I. Vigil, co-director with Bob Larsen of Team Running USA California. Coach Vigil showed up at my house in Tucson in an old, white Ford pickup. He and his wife, Caroline, had recently moved to Green Valley, Arizona, from his hometown of Alamosa, Colorado, where his Adams State College program had won 19 national championships and produced 425 All-Americans. Green Valley is 30 minutes south of Tucson, so I was right on the way—only 11 1/2 hours left to reach our destination!

Coach Vigil is well known throughout the sport as an engaging story-teller and a prankster. I had only talked to him briefly before our western adventure. We sped through the Sonoran and Mojave Deserts—Coach is not shy about the gas pedal—and by the time we reached US Route 395 and saw the Sierra Nevada range to the west and Death Valley to the east, I felt like we were old friends. We both had lots to talk about . . . me growing up in Somalia and Kenyan refugee camps and eventually learning a new country, him growing up poor in southern Colorado. One thing that stood out to me was how he didn't get into much trouble as a kid. I didn't either. In Mogadishu, some of us would try to go to the beach after lunch when we were supposed to be taking naps, but our parents usually won that battle. He had great respect for his single mother, and I had the same for my parents and what they had been through.

Mostly we talked about running. Coach Vigil has a doctorate in exercise physiology and had trained top distance runners at altitude since before I was born. The drive was like a seminar in the sport. He is extremely organized and analytical; I am not. In appearance and personality, we were an odd couple in that truck, but I had a great time. I think it surprised him to find out how much speedwork I was doing with Bernard Lagat, a 1500m runner. Lagat had followed his Washington State coach James Li to Tucson when Li took over as distance coach after Coach Murray retired from the University of Arizona. Coach Vigil told me later that he admired the way I could adapt to what other training partners were doing. He wanted to explain to his runners why they were doing a certain workout. Me? I just wanted to attack it—whatever it was. Coach Vigil and Coach Larsen were in contact with Coach Murray while I was in Mammoth. They weren't trying to change anything Coach Murray and I had planned. They just wanted to make sure we all stayed motivated, helped each other, and got the most out of our talents.

$$\mathcal{F} \; \mathcal{F} \; \mathcal{F}$$

Mammoth Lakes is one of those idyllic spots that looks almost fake until you're clicking off 15 sub-5:20 miles in a row at 8,000 feet above sea level. That's as real as it gets. The town is in the middle of nowhere—in a good way. The local airport didn't take commercial flights until 2009. Mammoth sits pretty much exactly halfway between San Francisco and Las Vegas. Lake Tahoe is three hours north up US Route 395; Yosemite National Park is two and a half hours away as you explore deep into the Sierra Nevada. Mammoth Lakes was founded as a gold-rush town in the 1870s, and it became a gold-rush town once again for Olympic hopefuls in the early 21st century, thanks in large part to what Coach Vigil and Coach Larsen created. With an elevation that sport scientists say is in the sweet spot for high-altitude training, and the committed investment of coaching experience and talent, Mammoth earned its reputation as one of the most desirable training spots in the country for endurance athletes.

Meb's success had Coach Murray and me thinking along the same lines as Coach Larsen and Meb, who had stayed together since Meb ran for him at UCLA, and Coach Vigil, who was Deena Kastor's coach: that I might also be a marathoner. David Monti, the elite athletes recruiter for the New York City Marathon, told me he thought I had the perfect stride for a marathoner. I shuffled along, looking deceptively slow, but in fact I was moving pretty quickly and conserving energy all the way. Deena and Meb both told stories of how after they finished their first marathons, they vowed never to do another. And now both had Olympic medals. I felt like I already had an advantage on them—I actually was excited to try out the longer distance!

In Deena's case, she originally trained for the marathon because Coach Vigil felt it would improve her endurance and toughness when she went back down to race the 10,000m. After earning the Olympic bronze, she never looked back, setting the still-standing American women's marathon record of 2:19:36 in 2006.

Their examples fueled my running. Even if I didn't take to 26.2 miles as we hoped, I expected benefits from the increased mileage and intensity of Mammoth training to transfer to the track.

🦌 🦌 🦌

Once Coach Vigil and I arrived, my first workout was September 18, a six-mile tempo run on Green Church Road, one of Mammoth's favorite stretches for runners. Ryan Shay, who had been here as Meb's training partner before Athens, was already there and as intense as ever.

Most of our workouts were lung-busters. The goal of the team environment was to push each other, not necessarily click off prescribed times each day. I loved it. Still, we were beating Meb pretty easily in 8- or 10-mile tempo runs for a few weeks. He had taken a couple weeks off after the Olympics, and it showed. I was feeling pretty good about handing it to an Olympic silver medalist each day. But Meb doesn't take long to get in shape, and soon he was running with us to get ready for the New York City Marathon.

I tweaked my Achilles tendon about three weeks out from New York and had to back off my mileage before I returned to Tucson (riding on a plane this time, next to someone who wasn't nearly the conversationalist Coach Vigil was). I was encouraged on October 29, nine days before New York. I ran a six-miler at 28:55, the last mile in 4:30. After nearly six weeks of living high, I was anxious for my first marathon, not sure what to expect.

All American eyes were on Meb, still basking in the glow of his silver medal. It seemed he was the country's hope to be a favorite at the 26.2-mile distance for years to come, yet he didn't show any stress. He was always gracious with the media and fans and seemed to enjoy having the target on his back.

Once in New York, I felt like I was royalty. Interview requests mostly went to Meb, but the excitement that he and the rest of us American runners were generating was noticeable in a race as famous as this one. I was rooting for Meb, but my Achilles was feeling better, and deep down I felt like I might pull a rabbit out of the hat and shock everyone with a debut under 2:10. Meb was incredibly supportive too. He told me I was in good enough shape to run a 2:08—and he meant it.

CHASING ABDI

From Go Be More podcast with Bryan Green and Jon Rankin, episode 28, July 17, 2020.

Jon: Your humility is one of your super powers. I was talking earlier to this fitness trainer and we were talking about gratitude as a super power. That's hand in hand with being humble. I see that as a strength of yours. I don't know if it's possible to make five Olympic teams and have a career span as long as yours without practicing those qualities wholeheartedly. You deserve everything you've gotten, brother. I'm excited to cheer for you.

Me: There's a lot that goes into running, but I'm thankful for everything I've got in life. I want to treat people the way I want to be treated. It's the little things that make a difference in life. It's not that hard. I also want to appreciate those recreational runners who run. They are the backbone of our sport. We are the only sport where our spectators are doing the same thing we're doing, only they're doing the harder thing. I run a marathon in 2:08 or 2:10. They run three or four hours. They are way tougher than I'll ever be. One of the things I don't like when I'm training is the long run. The long run will take you places you never go. Sometimes when I see people out there for three or four hours, I just want to go out and give them a hug and really appreciate them.

What really stood out about my first marathon was seeing how much people love to run. It's not that I didn't know that before. Back on Memorial Day weekend, Meb, Alan Culpepper, and I had won the International Team Challenge (and $45,000!) at the Bolder Boulder 10K, a big deal in a race that regularly features some of the best runners from Africa and everywhere else. That Colorado event, billed as the largest timed 10K in the world, is wild. The organizers do a great job—47,454 people partici-pated that year—and it's a big party.

But lining up with marathoners in New York felt even more like I was pulsing with their energy. First, it's New York City, and that's my favorite city on the planet. If you don't feel the energy of that place, you're not breathing. Second, it's a marathon, which means everybody there had to do some serious preparation to get to that point. And sure enough, tens of thousands of people were there with me, making the start at the Ver-razzano-Narrows Bridge shake. Sure, those of us at the front of the pack weren't going to see the masses as we ran through the five boroughs, but all of us were competing on the same course. I don't get to catch a pass at Gillette Stadium from Tom Brady or shoot a free throw at the Staples Center with LeBron James rebounding for me. Running is a democratic sport that welcomes all comers.

In New York that year, 36,513 runners crossed the same finish line in Central Park as I did. In fact, we "elites" get special treatment—trans-portation to the start line, hotel accommodations, no waiting lines to pee 15 minutes before the start, not to mention all the time to train and sleep and get massages and do yoga and get personal, top-level coaching in the weeks leading up to the race. Most of these people have to work in train-ing around work schedules and kids, not to mention buy their own shoes. But they do it for the love of the sport. They are the real heroes.

I felt strong through most of the race, but at 23 miles my injury began to flare up. I limped to the finish in 14th place with a partly torn Achilles tendon in a debut time of 2:17:09. One of the first people I saw was Monti, who had recruited me to the race. I told him, "I'm sorry. I want to come back and do this right." And I was not kidding around. I couldn't wait to come back and try again. Without a nagging injury and with greater respect for the distance—and knowledge of how to train for the distance without getting hurt—I was ready to push for a better time. Really, the pain of that distance was not much different than a 10,000m—you just had to keep going longer.

Meb didn't disappoint. He stuck with Hendrik Ramaala nearly all the way, until the South African pulled ahead in the final two miles for a victory in 2:09:28, just 25 seconds ahead of Meb. The only other American ahead of me was Ryan Shay, ninth in 2:14:08, who was one of my favorite training partners—and definitely my favorite cook—at Mammoth. I've never eaten food as good as the tofu soup he made when we lived together there. I don't know what he put in it, but it smelled and tasted so fresh. Ryan was developing into a true marathon talent under Coach Vigil, and he set a PR on the New York course that day.

It was encouraging to see how well the three of us did after training together. The camaraderie and energy among all the outstanding men and women runners at Mammoth was a true joy. Team Running USA California may have been designed to lift American distance-running performances, but it was also personally a breath of fresh air. For a guy like me who liked being in cities and thought I didn't want to be somewhere so remote for several months at a time, this was quite an admission to make.

This was also my first extended experience with altitude training. Tucson is just under a mile high, and it's easy to get from there to higher elevations, so I thought I was able to reap benefits that runners gained from training in places like Mammoth Lakes and Flagstaff in northern Arizona, where I also had been occasionally. By spending more time up high in Mammoth, though, I realized how taxing consecutive workouts were at 7,880 feet rather than at Tucson's 4,800 feet of elevation. I also enjoyed how I felt like I was flying when we would do speedwork in nearby Bishop, 4,150 feet high, while staying in Mammoth.

Coach Murray saw good things were happening for me, and even though my Athens race was sub-par, he was looking at the long game. Sure enough, I was as consistent as I could be over the next few years. I would see the Mammoth Lakes bunch, including my world cross country bronze medalist teammates Rogers, Downin, and Meb, at national and international competitions. Outstanding women runners like Deena, Amy Rudolph, Elva Dryer, and Jen Rhines kept doing well too.

$$\tilde{\jmath} \quad \tilde{\jmath} \quad \tilde{\jmath}$$

When Coach Vigil and I would talk in Mammoth Lakes, often at coffee shops, he was always so positive in his words. He was like that with everybody. He always projected more confidence in us than we had in ourselves. Coach Vigil knew what you were capable of and wanted to will you to see it too. As an athlete, when Coach Vigil says that to you, you take it and run with it. No one has ever accused me of having great foot speed, but with Coach Vigil, I could almost make myself believe that I do. Deena has credited him in her book and public speeches through the years for changing her mindset to one of success and positivity. I felt the same way with him.

I tell people that Coach Vigil is the coach of every distance runner of my generation. We all have our own coaches, but Coach Vigil is the one we all share. This is no disrespect to the many other smart and caring coaches I've met or worked with. I put Coach Vigil in a different category for several reasons. First, he's an exercise physiologist who has done his own research and read and applied sport science in ways that many of us take for granted. To be honest, I don't understand the physiological details of most of it and don't even really want to figure out why a lot of it works; I just know from experience that it does.

Second, with a few exceptions, I know runners are extremely generous with their knowledge and time. We aren't like football and basketball coaches who believe their game plans are state secrets or close off practices to the media and fans. Even among that kind group of people, Coach Vigil (along with Coach Larsen) took sharing to another level. He is an open book when it comes to training methods, strategy, anything at all, really. And he's curious and not cynical about the world, which meant he would ask me thought-provoking questions that surprised me. It was impossible to not feel comfortable around the guy. He's a great person, a good friend of mine, and a mentor to all runners. I bet I can name a hundred other people who would say exactly the same.

I would say a major part of why the Mammoth Lakes project turned out to be such a success is because coaches Vigil and Larsen made other coaches and sponsors comfortable with the idea that athletes could succeed in a team environment without losing their autonomy. There was no jealousy or whining about who got credit for a runner's success or which runners were getting more attention—and that mindset started at the top. I know Coach Murray trusted them entirely with the setup.

This attitude of trust extended to runners' schedules too. Coaches Vigil and Larsen allowed athletes like me to have flexibility to come and go. They knew I was doing the work when I was back in Tucson and was contributing when I was with them in California. Not all coaches would have considered that acceptable. Thankfully, I was able to go back and forth.

$$ \mathcal{Z} \ \mathcal{Z} \ \mathcal{Z} $$

I finished the 2005 season strong. At the World Championships in Helsinki, I placed 13th in 27:52.01. One of my favorite memories of that experience was a stopover in Oslo to run the 5000m at the Bislett Games as a tune-up for Helsinki. I'd never run in Oslo before, but the crowd was amazing. They screamed from the time the gun sounded until the last person crossed the finish line. I thought it was the mecca of distance running—and by that point I had been to a lot of cities that loved "athletics," as track and field is called throughout much of the world. They respect the sport.

The next night, Oslo impressed me again. Meb was a guest of honor at an Eritrean Festival, so he and his brothers invited me and our short-distance teammates David Krummenacker, Khadevis Robinson, and Jonathan Johnson to join them. I like to get out of the running zone sometimes, and this was the perfect way to do it. They treated us so well. We danced to Eritrean music, which reminded me of the fast-paced percussion and groovy rhythms of Somalia, and watched the Keflezighi brothers laugh and connect with people from their birth country.

It had been 12 years since I'd left Africa. I always made a point to speak Somali when I saw runners from Somalia and Swahili when I met runners from Djibouti, Kenya, and Tanzania at track meets around Europe and road races in the United States. It was fun to surprise guys who were new to the circuit and didn't expect me to speak African languages. I got to keep up with my skills, and it was usually good for a laugh (especially my Somali, which had dwindled by that point, especially after my family moved to Washington) and a connection point to build a relationship. But the Oslo festival was the first time I felt like I was actually in Africa, if only for a few hours in a corner of a big European city. I wondered when I might return to the continent where I was born.

I finished up the Scandinavian trip with another road win in September, the New Haven 20K in Connecticut (58:42), and knocked nearly six minutes off my marathon best (2:11:24) in my return to New York in November. I was thrilled, as I was less than two minutes behind the winner, Paul Tergat of Kenya, who outsprinted defending champion Ramaala. Meb reached the podium again with a third-place showing. I was fifth overall and had the leaders in my sight virtually the whole way.

By the end of 2005, I was sold on the value of altitude training, but I liked being in Arizona. I wanted the wisdom of Coach Murray but also that of Coach Vigil and Coach Larsen. I enjoyed my long workouts with Meb and my speed workouts with Kip in Tucson. I chose the best of all possible worlds and ended up spending a lot more time at a location that combined the best features of my other training grounds. It was like my own personal Mammoth Lakes in northern Arizona, a high-altitude spot with lots of trails easy to reach from Tucson. As it turned out, that third home would become an emotional and special place for me in my quest to make a third Olympics.

Second Olympic Ring

Athens

Back in Tucson after the 2000 Olympics, I was checking email, receiving congratulations and messages from friends and family. That's when I decided to change my email address to hakim2004@hotmail.com. This would be my daily reminder of my commitment to return to the next Olympics. To this day, that is my personal email—drop me a line to see if it's true! People ask me today why I still have "2004" in my email address. I've kept it because despite being known as a pretty laid-back guy, I ate up everything about my first Olympic experience. I wanted more, and this was when I shifted my perspective. I was on the move. For the first time in the sport, I was looking ahead. And I continued to improve under Coach Murray with hard work and decisions over the next four years leading up to the 2004 Olympics.

My Athens experience in 2004 was not so memorable on the track. That was the first year the 10,000m run didn't have a preliminary round, so we were a crowded, 24-man bunch circling the oval. I ran 28:26.26 to place 15th overall, a drop in place and time from my debut in Sydney.

Friends of mine from the University of Arizona definitely did have memorable showings, though. Jennie Finch was dominating as pitcher on the gold medal-winning U.S. softball team. In the pool, the South African 4x100m freestyle relay set a world record with three future or former U of A Wildcats, shocking a powerful American squad that included Michael Phelps. Ryk Neethling was the old man in that stunning upset. I want my fellow Americans to win, but I was thrilled for my good friend to reach that highlight in his incredible career filled with them.

Meb and Deena won medals as they followed the footsteps of the original marathon course—the 26-mile route from the battlefield of Marathon to Athens. In 490 BC, the Greek soldier Pheidippides is said to have run that distance to deliver the message that the Persians had been defeated. Legend has it that when he arrived in Athens, he said, "Joy, we win," just before collapsing of exhaustion and dying. Even I'm not sure I'm ready for that kind of dedication to the sport!

Sure, I would have liked to have finished higher, but I was not down about my race. I had qualified for another U.S. national team and made it to Athens—birthplace of the ancient and modern Olympics. Greece is pretty much unanimously called "the cradle of Western civilization," but there are several locations that claim the title of "cradle of civilization." Two of those influenced where I grew up: Egypt, just northwest of northern Somalia along the Red Sea, and Mesopotamia in modern-day Iraq, across the Gulf of Aden and the vast Arabian Peninsula. Many people spread across the Persian Gulf and east Africa over thousands of years from those two civilizations, leading to the hundreds of cultures, languages, religions, and clans that have developed, intermingled in, and unfortunately in some cases also devastated the region ever since. Somalia, on the edge of Arab and African worlds, Islam and Christianity, is a gateway to the interior of the African continent.

I like the sound of *cradle*. It's a comforting word—suggesting that something or someone is being nurtured so it can grow into something more mature . . . a present that is better than its past. What the word *cradle* doesn't tell you, though, is what the future will hold. That is for each of us to decide.

Whether as civilizations or individuals, progress toward becoming can feel slow, but isn't that really what we're all trying to do? Despite those tense times after 9/11, I found solace wherever I traveled during the early years of my pro career, from Helsinki to Hengelo, London to Lausanne, Monterey to Mammoth Lakes, and many points in between. Running was nurturing me by giving me purpose and helping me connect with others. My race times were improving, but more importantly, so was my appreciation of the world.

Part III
Beijing 2008

A LESSON IN BELIEF

"We all know Abdi the runner. He stumbled and fumbled his way into the sport. If that had never happened, the Abdi we know would not be much different. The core of Abdi is that he embodies a lot of things that we could use an injection of in our sphere and community and the world. He's a fun-loving, joyful person, but he's an incredibly loving, caring friend."

—Alicia Vargo, my Flagstaff friend

7

A BLACK CACTUS IN
THE PONDEROSA PINES

I spent much of my training cycle for the 2006 Chicago Marathon living in Flagstaff, Arizona. My neighbor was a jokester, and he knew I was a professional runner.

"Hey, man, you need a nickname," he said to me one day. "You should be 'Black . . . I don't know, Black something.'"

"Hell, no!" I shot back, laughing. "Not Black anything."

"Yeah, it would be great. I know: Black Saguaro. Or Black Cactus. You live in Tucson, so you're the Black Cactus!"

I smiled, humoring him: "OK, fine. Black Cactus."

I shrugged it off because distance runners aren't exactly known for having great nicknames. Can you think of any off the top of your head? I can't. People just go by their first name or some shortened version of their last name, right? Pre, Meb, Geb, Kip, Des, Mo, Shalane, Ritz. Other sports have awesome nicknames, but to me, it sounded arrogant for someone in my profession to have one. Yet over the next couple of weeks, I kept saying it over and over in my head, and to be honest . . . man, I loved it!

Everyone says you can't make your own nickname; that's just not how nicknames work. I did it anyway. I went back to Flagstaff after running Chicago—my first marathon that wasn't New York City. On that wonderful flat course, I set what remains my PR to this day: 2:08:56. Fourth place overall behind three Kenyans: 81 seconds behind winner Robert Kipkoech Cheruiyot, 76 seconds behind Daniel Nienga, and 65 seconds behind third-place Jimmy Muindi. I was feeling pretty bold when I got back to Flagstaff. A few days after returning to town, I saw Greg McMillan, the outstanding coach and founder of McMillan Running, who had a number of athletes training with him.

"Abdi," he said. "Great race in Chicago."

"Who is Abdi?" I replied. "I'm the Black Cactus."

Greg loved this and started calling me "Black Cactus" every chance he got. Others picked up on it, and I encouraged it. I thought, Why should I be self-conscious? It's a great name! I even started calling all the white American runners in town then "Black Cactus" just to keep it in circulation. They thought I did that because they all looked the same to me and I couldn't remember their names. Even more than Greg, the one who did more for spreading Black Cactus around town was the legendary Jack Daniels, who at that time was head distance coach at the Center for High Altitude Training at Northern Arizona University. Jack has this gruff voice anyway, and he never missed an opportunity to address me by my new name. I'd see him at the grocery store, or go to his office, or ride with him to a workout, and wherever we went, he'd say things like "How you feelin' today, Black Cactus?" or "Think you can handle the pace, Black Cactus?" It made me smile every time.

In so many ways, Flagstaff was quickly becoming a home away from Tucson for the Black Cactus.

$$\mathcal{F} \quad \mathcal{F} \quad \mathcal{F}$$

"Flag," as the locals call it, is sort of the other Arizona. Instead of giant humanoid saguaro cactuses, it's surrounded by the largest ponderosa pine forest in the world. It's a mountain town that gets more than 100 inches of snow per year—and I avoid that chilly side of Flagstaff whenever I can. But summer temperatures rarely get into the 90s, and summer monsoons arrive as sure as fireworks on the Fourth of July to drench the place until school starts. Runners have known this for a long time, but I have to correct lots of people who assume northern Arizona has 115-degree days, prickly pear, and Wile E. Coyote chasing the Road Runner. Those are only in the Sonoran Desert of southern Arizona . . . and Looney Tunes.

Flagstaff has been on the sports map since at least 1968, when preparation for the Olympics in Mexico City (7,200 feet) made Flagstaff's 7,000-foot elevation a desirable destination for many distance runners, including Jim Ryun, Billy Mills, and George Young. That has continued through the years, and especially around the turn of the century when elite endurance athletes began to embrace altitude training in greater numbers. They were coming from all over the world to train high in Flagstaff. Jack, who has a doctorate in exercise physiology, was a big reason for that. He is one of the world's foremost experts in altitude training, going all the way back to coaching Ryun before Mexico City. Flagstaff's high-altitude center received U.S. Olympic Training Site status in 2004 and Jack arrived in 2005. Having the stamp of the five rings and a guy *Runner's World* once called the "world's greatest running coach" move in brought even more top runners to town. Local residents were getting used to seeing fast runners on the roads, the extensive trail systems in and around the San Francisco Peaks and Mount Elden, and Buffalo Park, a scenic two-mile loop over open prairie in the middle of town.

I was a beneficiary of this trend. Through an initiative called "The Flagstaff Project," the Olympic training site would provide resources for top endurance athletes and promising young runners during their altitude stays. It wasn't an integrated team like Team Running USA California, but it provided tremendous support for lots of top runners who were trying to make it big. Money is still tight in distance running, but sponsorships and funding were really tough to find then. Ryan Shay, Anthony Famiglietti, and I were the first runners who received funding from The Flagstaff Project.

We were all free spirits. Fam, who is 100-percent New Yorker, was in the middle of two Olympic steeplechase appearances then. Fam is a blast. We'd talk about pretty much anything. Religion, food, why we run. He's told people, "Abdi? He's more American than you are." Sean Anthony, who was the associate director at the Center for High Altitude Training, said that some of his favorite memories of that time would be Fam and me rolling into the lobby or Sean's office around the same time and just trading jabs back and forth. "You guys should have your own talk show," he said.

Fam created a homemade movie called "Run Like Hell" during that time that was kind of wild. I'm in it, and I still don't really know what to say other than that it's like his training sessions, his philosophy of running, and an hour-long music video all rolled into one. I agree with a lot of what he says in it. He talks about how much he loves to punish his body in workouts and then take his easy days very easy. And he says you have to surround yourself with people who keep you motivated or you won't continue. I definitely relate to the final words in the documentary: "Don't take it too seriously. Just run like hell."

In his film, Fam shows himself joining Kip Lagat and me for a four-mile tempo run in Flagstaff. After a 4:30 mile, Kip pulls away, then I put a gap between Fam and me until he reels me in over the final half mile. When we're back in his car, Fam asks me how it felt to get outkicked. I look over at him and glare as though he just insulted my family. Too soon, man; too soon.

I cut him some slack for that, though, because he also filmed me showing off my 22-inch wheels on my Denali: "Rolling on 'twenties,' baby,'" I say. "Twenties from the factory. You've never seen these before." I loved driving that beast around. Fam also shows himself playing golf inside Kip's condo and his bulldog, Piggy, picking a fight with another dog at the trailhead. Kip and his wife, Gladys, adopted Piggy in Flagstaff; Gladys used to give me a hard time because I always wanted to take Piggy for walks. "You're just using my dog to strike up conversations with women," she said.

Starting in 2004, Kip and I made April 1 our annual pilgrimage from Tucson to Flagstaff. We wanted the altitude, but we both hated the cold. By April Fool's Day, we were usually safe. I spent time in Flagstaff before the 2004 Olympics and during my successful 2005 season, which included a win in the U.S. Men's 10-Mile Road Championships in Louisville, Kentucky. Six weeks later, I ran my fastest 10,000m on the track to date in Hengelo, The Netherlands: 27:33.47. It felt effortless, in flow, surely the easiest race I ever ran in my whole life. I was ready to race with anyone. The U.S. Championships in Carson, California, less than a month later, determined the national team for the World Championships in Helsinki, Finland. I held off Meb in a sprint to the finish to win the national title in 28:10.38, nineteen-hundredths of a second ahead of my roommate. We figured the two of us would be the ones pushing the pace, and we did. For five miles we worked together, and then we were on our own. I cherished our rivalry for many years, no matter the outcome. Any professional runner during Meb's time knows how hard it was to beat him. I didn't always do it, but I did that day.

I was feeling more and more comfortable in Flagstaff. I have never changed my official residence, but Jack, Sean, Fam, and many others in the running community have always made Flag feel special.

For me, professionally, Flagstaff—four hours from Tucson—offered convenient altitude training with tons of training partners to choose from. I loved it. I really hadn't been to Flagstaff much until this time. I have not run a lot of indoor miles in my career, but in college I ran a 4:21.8 at Walkup Skydome in 1999. Ron Mann was the NAU coach back at that time, and when I would see him in later years, including the 2005 Helsinki World Championships when he was the U.S. men's team coach, he joked with me that I should have become a Lumberjack rather than a Wildcat.

One time, he was asked about his first impression of me. "You can't miss Abdi's smile," he said. To be honest, I can't think of a better way I would want somebody to answer that question about me. It makes a guy feel pretty good.

Flagstaff in 2006 was when I really started taking the possibility of becoming a marathoner seriously. I placed third at the New York Nike Half Marathon in August (1:01:34) and second at the Philadelphia Half (1:01:07) as tune-ups for my fall marathon in Chicago. It had been a breakthrough season. I had the best American times that year in the 10K (27:22.81, in Hengelo, The Netherlands), the half (in Philly), and the marathon (Chicago). Coach Murray and I decided if I was going to make a third Olympic team, it might just be in the marathon this time.

$$\mathcal{F} \; \mathcal{F} \; \mathcal{F}$$

As the number of elite American distance runners increased in the early 2000s, I was noticing that more Americans were running from the front. That may sound obvious or like it's one and the same thing: C'mon, Abdi, you might say, more Americans were running from the front because they were good enough to do it. In years where they couldn't keep up, they were by definition in the middle or back of the pack. But I don't buy that argument. I would respond to you that once Americans realized other Americans could sustain a punishing pace, more Americans took a leap of faith that they could too. I fully believe Meb and I were important in changing that mindset. Coach Murray encouraged it. I didn't take the approach that my happiness was just based on finishing top 20 or beating a certain number of other Americans. I wanted to run with the best for as long as I could. If I blew up, fine; at least I went for the win.

Racing—and training—is a psychological mind-bender. Running can devastate a person or it can give them an opportunity to reach deeper and come out the other side stronger. Take me, as an example. Once the snow melted in Flagstaff and Tucson started to heat up, Kip and I would head to Flag. Coach Murray and Kip's coach, James Li, encouraged us to work out together several times a week even though we were in different events.

We often ran Old Walnut Canyon Road, but I sometimes liked to join Kip—a two-time Olympic 1500m medalist at that time, don't forget—on his workouts at the Lumberjack Stadium track. This may sound crazy for me, a 10,000m runner and marathoner, to do, but Kip always brings out the best in me, so even if it wasn't in my plans, sometimes I would do it. Jack Daniels told this story when he was interviewed for the documentary "Running Away to Flagstaff":

> One day Abdi, he asked me to time him. Bernard was there, and so they were going to do some six hundreds. This was unbelievable

because Bernard's going to kill Abdi in the shorter stuff. But they did 'em together. They'd do a 600 and just jog diagonally back across the football field to the start to do the next one. They weren't getting very much rest. Bernard was running these things pretty darn fast. So every one of 'em, Bernard would beat Abdi by about six or seven seconds. They did six of them, I think. After six of them, Bernard says, 'OK, that's good, we're done.' Abdi says, 'Nah, I think I'll do another six.' He was getting beat so bad that he had to show him up by doing six more.

You think I liked getting crushed by Kip over and over? Of course not. But I knew it was making me better. Some people don't want to look bad in front of others, even in training. But I wasn't embarrassed by it. In fact, I wanted to make sure one of the best friends I've ever had—a guy I love and trust more than just about anybody else in the world—knew he hadn't broken me.

CHASING ABDI

Kip isn't the only Olympic medalist that pushed me on the NAU track through the years...

"It's hard to keep that competitive edge. In 20 years of racing, I've never seen him panic or quit. What you see is what you get. Even the past few years when I look out my office window [at Lumberjack Stadium] and see him with Mo [Farah] and watch him getting dropped. Many athletes wouldn't put up with that. The only way you do that is if you're dialed in to what *you* are doing. He's seeking out a challenging psychological scenario and using it to his advantage. It speaks to a mindset that has served him well."

—Mike Smith, Director of Track and Field and Cross Country, Northern Arizona University

Anybody who has run with me knows how seriously I take my job and also how much fun I have doing it. Again, that can be a mind-bender. I had run against and with Ryan Shay ever since college. He ran for Notre Dame while I was at Arizona, and we got to know each other well when he and I stayed in the same condo at Mammoth. Ryan was also a frequent visitor to Flagstaff, and in January 2007, he and his fiancée, Alicia Craig, an All-American runner herself from Stanford, moved to Flag full time. Alicia and Ryan, as well as I and lots of other runners, lived at Mike Smith's tiny rental house. Like Ryan and me, Mike was preparing for the Olympic Trials. He had moved to Flagstaff the year before, and everybody knew they could crash at Mike's for a few days or weeks. He had bodies on couches and in his garage, any open space available. With so many runners wanting to come to town and rentals hard to come by, Mike's generosity really helped make it work for a lot of us.

I don't know how many couples would willingly live with a dozen other people coming in and out like that, and I think Ryan and Alicia realized they needed some space. They moved into their own house a couple months later. That worked out well for me, too, because they invited me to stay with them when I was in town. I couldn't have chosen a better home for being a third wheel. They welcomed me warmly . . . well, Alicia did. I think Ryan had his doubts sometimes!

I've been a running vagabond a lot of my career, but Ryan was my main training partner in summer 2007. I had a blast, but it could get intense. I don't always stick with my plan on a given day. We might start on a 10-mile recovery run, but if I was feeling strong, I'd push a little harder. Ryan didn't dare tell me to dial it back. Instead, he'd go faster too. I'd respond. Pretty soon, we were both getting closer to race pace than we ever should have, but there was no giving in now. I had turned an easy day into a hard progression workout. And other than some mumbled curse words from Ryan—he was a prolific cusser—none of this was spoken. We'd return to the house and Alicia would know exactly what had happened. Ryan was scowling. I was beaming. He was exhausted and furious that he had taken my bait. I was exhausted and happy I'd gotten under his skin.

It wasn't just Ryan. In Flagstaff, every day was a new challenge, a new view, and a new guy to tease. You never have to run the same route twice in that town. Tempo runs with Bernard off Old Walnut Canyon Road near Coach Mann's house. Long days with Andrew Lemoncello on endless Lake Mary Road. Without a doubt, though, A1 Mountain Road Loop is the best of Flagstaff's many options. In my opinion, if you haven't done the 21-mile A1 loop, you've never really been to Flagstaff—seven miles up, seven miles around the top, and seven miles back down. When I was getting ready for Chicago, I remember one day where I clicked off 5:10 miles the whole way. Greg McMillan was on a bike beside me, and I think he was pretty impressed.

Alicia once told an interviewer that I was the definitive "king of A1 Mountain Road." She said, "I can remember watching him, his head hanging sideways, drool hanging out of his mouth, snot coming out of his nose, just to set the course record for A1 Mountain Road."

I loved that Alicia would put up with me and that Ryan was willing to play my mental games. Like me with Kip, Ryan was not going to admit I had broken his spirit. Like Meb and me, he was a rare exception during that period—an American runner who would stay with the front pack and run like hell not to get dropped. It wasn't by accident that the three of us were among the favorites in the Olympic Trials.

8

SOME DAYS ARE BETTER THAN OTHERS

I had two big dates coming up in late 2007—and both were in my favorite city.

Sure, the U.S. Championships and, if I qualified again, the World Championships loomed. But 2007 was a quirky year. The U.S. Olympic Trials for the men's marathon were held early in the 2008 Olympic cycle in order to be paired with the annual New York City Marathon. The Trials were on Saturday, November 3, 2007, with more than 100 men running a loop course through Central Park. The next day, nearly 40,000 runners would participate in the traditional route that meandered through the whole city. It was planned as a weekend extravaganza for the sport.

I would do all I could to prepare for the Worlds, of course. But the Olympics always got my juices flowing, and I was more prepared to make the team than I had been in my two previous Olympic attempts.

To get ready for the Trials in November, I would compete again in the NYC Half in August, where I had placed third in 2006. It's a tough, hilly half-marathon course—some of it in Central Park—that would be useful to experience again before the full marathon at the Trials. Plus, you know . . . it's New York.

But first things first. Coming off a marathon personal best in Chicago late in 2006, I had a golden opportunity to make my first trip back to Africa since I was a kid. The World Cross Country Championships were being held in March in Mombasa, Kenya, of all places, the same city where I had been in a refugee camp. It seemed fitting that I would return under such different circumstances.

But you have to get the job done to qualify, and even though I was considered a strong contender at the U.S. Championships, I didn't. A documentary called "Showdown" focused on me and four others—Alan Culpepper, Dathan Ritzenhein, Jorge Torres, and Meb—preparing for the race. I guess it was a day for the hometown runners. The top four finishers in Boulder that day were University of Colorado alumni: Culpepper, followed by Adam Goucher, Ritzenhein, and Torres. I finished two minutes back in 21st place.

As my favorite rock band, U2, sang:

Some days it all adds up,
And what you got is not enough.
Some days are better than others.

That summer of 2007 as I trained with Ryan, though, I was on fire. Back at Hengelo, I hung with the leaders at Blankers-Koen Stadion. We passed the halfway mark of the 10,000m in 13:28, ahead of the pace to break Meb's American record (27:13.98), and I felt strong. I got a side stitch and faded to 13th in 27:31.46, but I was aggressive the way I always want to be. Then, in the span of 24 days, I won three races, including the 10,000m on the track at the U.S. Championships and the prestigious Atlanta Peachtree Road Race on the Fourth of July.

One month after Peachtree, I ran what I still call my best race ever. Most of the attention at the New York Nike Half—rightfully so—was on Haile Gebrselassie, who had won all seven half marathons he had ever entered and was running for the first time under the spotlight of New York City. He was still in his prime. He had set his 22nd world record just a month earlier, and a year before, he had become the first man to run a half marathon under 59 minutes.

I knew what I was capable of, though. I thought back to the 10,000m I ran in Hengelo just two months earlier and knew that with my recent training and racing, I was in better shape than I had been in 2006 when I took third in the inaugural New York Half.

I was willing to challenge anybody, even possibly the greatest of all time—even the guy who blew past me in my first Olympics and had me watching the video screen at his gold-medal performance a few laps later.

With all due respect to Haile, I told Weldon Johnson of LetsRun.com, "If I knew Haile was going to beat me in the race, if I knew Haile was going to win and I had no chance I wouldn't have come. I'm not running for second place. I'm running to win."

I meant it, too. I live for the chase, and I'm not afraid to get out of my comfort zone.

Already by mile five, three of us had broken the race open before we had even left Central Park: Haile, Robert Cheruiyot (who was two-time defending Boston Marathon and defending Chicago Marathon champ at the time), and me. Soon after the halfway point, I surged and decided to take the race to Geb. I even told them, "Go," as I did it, urging them to join me. That burst was enough to drop Cheruiyot, but Geb still had plenty left in the tank. He passed me with five miles to go, and I was chasing him the rest of the way to Times Square. I probably played into his hands by pushing so hard, and the toll it took may have cost me a sub-60-minute time, but I was all smiles afterward. I felt like my best chance was to catch him off guard. Besides, how many people get to tell their future kids that they went toe to toe with Haile Gebrselassie?

I found out that in a prerace press conference, Haile had singled me out as the one who would offer him the best competition. And after the race was over, he said, "Abdi at this time is a very good athlete like me, the very top."

At the end of the day, I set a personal best by nearly 40 seconds (1:00:29) on a hilly, humid course, and it took a 59:24 from the world's best to beat me. It was the third-fastest half ever by an American (though the point-to-point course means it doesn't get considered an official mark), but my time was actually only the second fastest in 2007. Ryan Hall had run a stunning 59:43 in Houston to start the season. But, hey, I already told you: I'm not trying to be the fastest American; I'm trying to be the fastest runner! Here's what I said after the race:

"I made a surge. I dropped Cheruiyot, but Haile is the greatest runner ever, man. I have total respect for him. He's still at the top of his game. I gave it my best . . . That was the plan to see who would come with me. I ended up second. Getting second to him, the greatest distance runner of all time, I'm not ashamed, but I wanted to win the race.

"I've been successful the last couple of years. I've always been up there with one of the best 10Ks in the U.S., which is not my goal. My goal is to run one of the best 10Ks in the world."

Nothing in New York that day made me second-guess my choice of favorite city.

I placed seventh in the 10,000m at Nagai Stadium in Osaka, Japan, three weeks later—my highest-ever finish on the track at a World Championships. A month before the men's U.S. Olympic Marathon Trials, I won another race: the Twin Cities 10-Mile in St. Paul, Minnesota, in a time of 47:34. I tweaked my hip in the victory, but I was able to keep moving. A few days of rest, and I'd be back on track for the Trials.

CHASING ABDI

Abdi's Running Rules to Live By

1. A setback is a setup for a comeback.

2. There is no such thing as a quick fix.

3. The last week of a taper cannot make you fitter.

4. Recovery is part of your training.

5. Have fun and enjoy the journey.

—From The Physical Performance Show podcast interview, episode 221, June 26, 2020

To be honest, many times in my running career I've felt like the underdog. Maybe most athletes feel that way, but you can definitely psych yourself out if you worry about not getting the respect you think you deserve. When I've been an underdog, I've used that to my advantage, seeing it as an opportunity to show others how good I can be.

In late 2007, though, I could no longer be considered an underdog. With the U.S. Olympic Trials looming, I had improved in each of the three marathons I'd run, and I had two consecutive years of solid times across distances from 6.2 miles to 26.2 miles. And the race would be held partially on a course I had just recently crushed. U2's "Some Days are Better Than Others" came to mind again:

Some days are sulky, some days have a grin
And some days have bouncers and won't let you in.

There have been plenty of times in my life when I felt locked out, but on my return trip to New York City in 2007, I didn't see any bouncers . . . and I was grinning. Everything seemed aligned to make November 3, 2007, a memorable day.

I always respect anybody who lines up for the same race as me, but my confidence ahead of that marathon was through the roof. Back in August, just after my second-place finish in the half, I was looking ahead to the marathon course in an interview with LetsRun.com. "The small hills of Central Park, I think they will favor me as I don't have that much weight to carry," I said. "I'm a lean mean machine. That's why I call myself the Black Cactus."

Yep, the Black Cactus was leaving the ponderosa pines and the altitude of Flagstaff to return to the city of skyscrapers I loved to run underneath. The Big Apple was the biggest stage in the sport, and I—along with my fellow Flagstaff qualifiers—was ready to take a bite.

9

THAT'S WHERE
I LOST YOU . . . NEW YORK

The start line before a marathon is a quiet place. It's even more so at a small marathon where every competitor is capable of running in the two-teens and has the exact same goal: finish in the top three. At the Olympic Trials, personal records can wait for another day.

Other than head nods and some scattered "good lucks," there's nothing left for anybody to say. We're all in our own heads or fidgeting with our watches, getting ready for the biggest day of our work lives, which only comes around once every four years.

Even in that solitude, Ryan Shay and I made eye contact on a perfect New York November morning—crisp, barely 50 degrees—waiting for the gun to go off on Fifth Avenue outside St. Patrick's Cathedral.

"Believe in yourself," I said to him, echoing words he and I had uttered to each other many times over the past half year.

It's funny to me, thinking back on how many different conversations those three words had launched. We each had accomplished so much as runners, and yet we both needed to hear the reminder regularly. From the outside, I'm guessing that would surprise people. I like to goof around, not get too serious. That attitude can make it seem like I'm worry-free and always sure about what I'm doing. Ryan was intense, serious, and he would never admit weakness in a workout or a conversation. That could come across as arrogant, but it certainly seemed like he was sure of himself. Believing in ourselves didn't seem to be a problem for either of us.

Of course we struggled at times with confidence, though. We're humans, aren't we?

Here I was, a thin two-time Olympian from Somalia who liked to crack jokes, considered a natural talent, who made my plans on the fly.

Here he was, a stocky guy from Michigan who fought to become an Olympian and was driven by a desire to prove to others he was worthy of success. He was disciplined in adhering to the training plans Coach Joe Vigil gave him for many years.

Ryan and I never argued. We both found out early on, when we were housemates at Mammoth Lakes, that there was no point. When his mind was made up, there was no way you were going to change it. I called it "Ryan's way." That worked out well for me, because I have no desire to argue with anybody. I don't try to change other people's opinions, and I make sure other people aren't pushing their opinions on me. I'll say my two cents and I want to listen to yours. If we don't see eye to eye, we can still be friends or we can part ways. But I won't waste my time or yours trying to make you see the world my way.

We sometimes disagreed, but it would be completely forgotten after the moment passed. I'm not going to lose sleep over a difference of opinion, and Ryan knew he could say anything to me without harming the friendship. This meant we could be vulnerable with each other. We looked and acted so differently, but we burned with the same fire inside. I got nervous before big races. He had complex reasons for wanting to win, always wanting to prove he was worthy of respect and love. He'd bust on me, asking when I was going to win a medal or break an American record. I'd remind him that running—even in a punishing tempo run or mile repeats—could be done with a laugh. The mark of any great friendship is that two people believe in each other, and that continually restores their belief in themselves. Ryan and I definitely had that.

Best of all, he talked about how amazing Alicia was. I saw how much her sweetness had softened his rough exterior. When it came to running, he was as tough as ever. But I can tell you she gave him an inner peace that was not there before he met her two years earlier. I got to see all of this happen in real time as they became accustomed to their new home in Flagstaff and as they prepared for their July wedding.

When Ryan and Alicia got married in 2007, it was a big deal in the growing Flagstaff running community. Sara Hall, an elite runner married to one of the Olympic Trials marathon favorites, Ryan Hall, was one of Alicia's bridesmaids. They had all been friends since their Stanford days and, like me, had all spent time at Mammoth and now in Flagstaff. Even after the wedding, with big races piling up and me wanting to stay at altitude, Ryan and Alicia were fine with letting me continue to crash with them. Because of the kindness of two newlyweds, I saw each day in their new house what a loving relationship looked like.

When we took the shuttle to the start line, the sun was still asleep. Pretty much everybody had climbed inside. Ryan and Alicia walked toward the bus in the darkness and gave each other a hug. Ryan hopped on board.

🏃 🏃 🏃

When the gun went off, I was locked in. I believed in myself, and I had no doubt Ryan believed in the possibilities for the day as well. From St. Patrick's, we took a six-block detour to the south, past Rockefeller Center, and then turned onto Seventh Avenue for a mile before entering Central Park, where we would spend the rest of the morning.

It didn't take too long, unfortunately, for me to realize that the hip flexor that bothered me in Minnesota belied my self-confidence. I tried to stay in contention while not putting too much stress on it, but that's hard to do when you're running close to five-minute miles, one after the other. My body was made to withstand that kind of stress, I thought, but not today. It was flaring up, and I knew finishing the race was only risking further damage. I decided to shut myself down at about 18 miles, around 102nd Street, the northernmost section on the fourth lap through the park.

I was stunned. So much preparation, all for nothing. In a disappointed daze, I wasn't focused on much of anything. Somehow, I returned to the staging area and gathered my things. I had no idea what was happening in the race. The leaders were well out of sight when I stopped, and to be honest, I didn't care to see who made the team. I have only dropped out of a few races in my whole career, but normally, even on a rough day I bounce back quickly and catch up with my friends and competitors. This time, I got on the shuttle to go back to the hotel.

I slumped in my seat as we started to move. Another runner near me, Peter Gilmore, looked devastated. His eyes made contact with mine and he shook his head. "I can't believe it," he said. It wasn't even 9:30 in the morning. He must have had a tough day too.

"I can't believe Ryan is gone," Peter said.

I was confused. "What do you mean?"

He told me that Ryan Shay had died. The words didn't compute in my head. Ryan DNF'd . . . right? That's what "died" meant. Where is he now?

No, he explained. Ryan collapsed, and they were unable to revive him. Ryan was gone. We soon learned the details that the rest of the world was discovering. About 5 1/2 miles into the race, near the Central Park boathouse, Ryan went down. He was given immediate medical attention and then taken to Lenox Hill Hospital, where he was pronounced dead at 8:46 a.m. While I had been deciding whether to end my race, medical staff had been striving in vain to revive my 28-year-old friend.

Cause of death was cardiac arrhythmia from an enlarged heart. He apparently had known about it since he was a teenager but never complained about it. Ryan didn't want to stop running, and he didn't want to make excuses.

I thought back to the morning. As we warmed up beside each other, I didn't suspect anything was wrong. I'm pretty sure I was the last person to talk to him. Near the halfway point of the race, I actually looked around for him, figuring he must be near me. We had run too many miles together for him not to be right there pushing me, telling me to get my skinny ass in gear.

$$\mathcal{Z} \ \mathcal{Z} \ \mathcal{Z}$$

Putting a bad race behind me is not a problem. Within a day or two, I'm ready to move on. Some days are better than others, right? Losing a great friend is another story. Even in Somalia, the deaths that I saw or heard about were not people I was close to. My parents may have known them, or they were distant relatives, but to a teenage boy they were just names. In the weeks that followed Ryan's death, I didn't want to run and I didn't want to discuss what happened. Ryan had so much ambition and outworked everybody. For several months, I had envisioned Ryan and me discussing Beijing together that winter, knowing we both had reached our goal of making the Olympic team. I didn't think anybody or anything was capable of stopping him.

Jack Daniels had a big ping-pong tournament planned for his house once the Flagstaff contingent returned from the Trials. Now, nothing seemed important.

I spoke at Ryan's funeral, but I barely remember the day. With the weather starting to turn cold in Flag, I stayed in Tucson. That wasn't unusual for me. I always spent the winter where it was warmer. But if I was honest with myself, I didn't want to be in Flagstaff. There was nothing I could say that would console Alicia or anybody else there who loved Ryan. Even though Alicia and Ryan had graciously opened their home to me, now it was the last place I felt comfortable.

If I was unwilling to spend time in her house, imagine how she felt. And yet, she persevered. Alicia showed all of us a path toward healing. She put her own Olympic dreams on hold, realizing she needed to welcome her grief rather than push it down. No one in Flagstaff would have blamed her if she had moved away from town. She slowly began to smile again, accepting invitations to dinner and using running as a way to connect with others. We saw her struggle and survive—and when we did, it gave us a chance to follow along.

Alicia and I have never talked much about that day. We know what is in each other's hearts. Before long, I stayed with her in that house again. She continued to host me for years when I was in Flagstaff—even if I called her 30 minutes outside of town while driving to ask. She has hosted many runners through the years, including lots of Africans who come through for altitude-training camps. Alicia is one of the biggest cheerleaders for Flagstaff because of how much support she received there when she experienced tragedy. She and her dog Tanner bounding through the Peaks as she resumed her running career on the trails became an emblem of Flagstaff resilience. Alicia has since remarried, to an excellent runner named Chris Vargo. Running is an important part of their lives, and they are a beloved part of the community.

I don't really allow myself to have regrets—regrets lead to stagnation because you can't change what has already happened. Really, what we consider regret is usually just an opportunity to grow. Still, I have to admit, I wish I had been more available to Alicia. Recently, she talked to a friend about me, and it gave me great peace of mind about the months that followed Ryan's death. With her permission, I'm sharing it here:

When you lose somebody, you quickly see the character of the people you're surrounded by. It gives you this enormous gratitude for the people who are there for you. They're solid and they're not afraid of what you're walking through. There's a depth of character that comes through. Through the loss of Ryan, the care and compassion from Abdi, I'm forever grateful for that. How he cared not just about Ryan but how he took care of me out of loyalty to Ryan. That has nothing to do with how fast he runs. But the faster he runs, the more people see that in him. He's a shining light in the sport. Abdi's a good man. That's something that is hard to express from my position, but I've been in some very difficult, dark places in my life. I'm so glad God put an Abdi in my life. When I do see him, I know if I ever need anything, Abdi would be there and do something for me at the drop of a hat. Because Ryan was such a dear friend and he'd do anything for him, and I'm an extension of that.

꙳ ꙳ ꙳

For the first couple months after the Trials, it was hard to think about running. When I did, I remembered how much Ryan wanted to become an

Olympian. I never want to presume what someone would want for me. I knew Ryan very well, but I can't possibly know that for certain. Fortunately, I stayed in touch with Ryan's brothers, Nathan and Stephan, and they became a source of support. Stephan told me Ryan would want all of us to keep doing what we love, and it was hard to argue with that simple statement. I felt like Stephan gave me permission to start thinking ahead to the Olympic Track and Field Trials. My marathon didn't go as planned, to say the least. But the 10,000m was still a pathway to the 2008 Beijing Olympics.

During training, I talked to Ryan in my head. I thought about what good partners we were. Alicia said he and I had a "perfect marriage," which may sound weird coming from his wife, but I think it was accurate. We may have seemed like oil and water, but we both gained so much from our time together. I think Ryan wanted sometimes to not take himself so seriously, but it was ingrained in him. He was a collegiate champion, a national champion on the roads, an economics major who finished top of his class from one of the country's best universities. Ryan was driven and successful in everything he did. But it came at a cost. He felt the world was on the line with every workout and race. Sometimes he lost the joy that should be part of accomplishing great things. I hope I helped bring some fun into his life.

But Ryan gave me just as much. I don't like arguing. I'll do whatever I can to avoid that tension. He let me say what was on my mind, knowing disagreement didn't mean a breakup. He always knew what I needed to hear that would lift me up when I was nervous or felt unseen in the world. It could be a kick in the butt or a word of encouragement . . . actually, it was usually a kick in the butt! But he paid attention. He cared. He always gave me respect and was always there for me. Anybody who was close to him understood that. Even now, I carry that experience with me every day.

Thanks to Ryan, I was on a mission in 2008. At the Monument Avenue 10K in Richmond, Virginia, I won. At the Prefontaine Classic—named after another gritty runner who died much too young—I set what remains my personal best in the 10,000m with a 27:16.99. Back in Eugene, Oregon, on the Fourth of July a month later, I led from start to finish at the Olympic Trials in the 10,000m. I dared anyone to go with me and held off hometown star Galen Rupp, who was still at the University of Oregon. Qualifying for a third Olympics after all that had happened in the past seven months was exhilarating. I felt pure joy. There's no other way to describe it. I didn't know what to do with myself. I barely slowed down after hitting the tape and just kept rolling into a victory lap, slapping hands with fans in the front row all the way around. Finally, when I got to the steeplechase water jump at Hayward Field, I just walked into the middle of it and lay down on my back like I was getting into a bathtub and looked straight up into the sky. It was cleansing. I only wish Ryan had been there, too.

CHASING ABDI

This tweet included a GIF of the steeplechase bath from NBC Sports' coverage of the 2008 Trials. I can't recreate that 14 seconds of video here in a book, but replacing it with this photo of a wet, happy Olympian says it all.

Photo © Pat Holleran

🐦 **Andrew Carlson**
@ACarlson701

5 Olympic Teams and far too many accolades to cover in a single tweet...but this remains as my top @Abdi_runs moment of all time.

7:14 PM · Jan 25, 2021·Twitter for iPhone

🐦 **Gary Allen**
@garyallen262

Jan 26

Replying to

@ACarlson701
and
@Abdi_runs

THE Black Cactus don't see much water out on the desert!

🐦**D Nukuri**
@DDNukuri

Jan 26

🐦**Axel Wheeler - Long-Haul Trucker for Hire**
@Schlegality

Jan 26

Replying to
@ACarlson701
and
@Abdi_runs

I was there and saw the race!! 2008 Olympic 10K trials. Imagine qualifying to represent the US on dang 4th of July, with fireworks and everything immediately following your victory.

🐦**Evan Day**
@edayrun

Jan 26

Replying to
@ACarlson701
and
@Abdi_runs

Long live the Black Cactus!

—Tweet from Andrew Carlson, former professional runner and current North Dakota State University cross country coach, January 25, 2021, with a sampling of replies

❦ ❦ ❦

Ever since Ryan's funeral, I had been wearing a black rubber wristband that read, "Believe in yourself." Those final three words between Ryan and me were important to keep close during that period. They're worth remembering when everything seems to be in your favor on a given day and yet you don't succeed—then come back on a better day to do just that. When you doubt you can keep up with other people. When tragedy makes you wonder whether you want to do even the things that make you happy.

If U2 spoke truth to me with kind of a goofy song like "Some Days are Better Than Others," they did so even more with a somber song, "New York," that they wrote shortly after 9/11.

That's where I lost you ... New York.
In New York I lost it all to you and your vices
Still I'm staying on to figure out my midlife crisis
I hit an iceberg in my life
But you know I'm still afloat
You lose your balance, lose your wife
In the queue for the lifeboat.

New York is still my favorite city to visit. Within three months in 2007, it gave me the highest running high and the lowest personal low I've ever had. It could have been a bittersweet place after the Olympic Marathon Trials, but that's not how I saw it. The site of Ground Zero and Ryan's death is also home to the most diverse, dynamic city in the world and the United Nations. The site of my DNF is also the site of my best race. I embrace all of it. I still get excited to go there, and in fact I returned to the New York City Marathon in November 2008 as part of a group we created called Team Shay that ran in honor of Ryan.

New York City takes in all the celebrations and the burdens of the world, and I love it for that. But you know what? Watching Alicia's journey, I found out that in its own way, so does Flagstaff.

Third Olympic Ring

Beijing

E verything the hosts did at the 2008 Olympics was over the top, and I was grateful to be part of it. Some of it didn't make sense to me. It felt strange when the distance runners flew to Dalian for a day of training and they actually shut down the roads in a city of millions just for us to run a few miles. Ron Mann, the former Northern Arizona University coach then at Louisville, was our middle-distances coach, and it was fun to reconnect with him.

One of the most amazing experiences was the Opening Ceremonies. That is always a highlight of the Olympics, of course, but that night the entire American team was led into the quirky stadium known as the Bird's Nest by 1500-meter runner Lopez Lomong.

When Lopez was just six years old growing up in Sudan, rebel soldiers took him from his family while they were at church. Getting help from some older boys who were also kidnapped, he literally had to run for his life to escape to a Kenyan refugee camp. Lopez was there for years as one of the "Lost Boys" of Sudan before being adopted by an American family just before 9/11, which shut down that refugee program. He was an NCAA champion at NAU and, a year before the Beijing Games, he became a U.S. citizen.

I could certainly relate to leaving my home country as a child because of civil war, finding a new life in Kenya and the United States, and getting help from strangers along the way. As part of the track team, I knew Lopez enough to know he was a great guy even beyond his incredible story, so it was easy for me to vote for him to be flag bearer. I was thrilled that so many more of the 588 athletes across all sports on the U.S. Olympic contingent agreed that he deserved to carry the Stars and Stripes into the Bird's Nest.

I didn't perform particularly well at the 2008 Olympics. I equaled my 15th place finish from 2004 with a time of 27:52.53. Maybe I kept training too hard after qualifying, rather than backing off. Maybe the emotions of the year finally caught up with me. Still, my first trip to China was a memorable experience. I had transitioned from sorrow to a renewed dedication to running, but I wasn't sure where my future in the sport lay. The past two years, I had run faster and in more types of races than ever in my life. But I was now 31 years old. Maybe the roads were calling for good.

A new face on the University of Arizona campus.
(University of Arizona Athletics)

The second of many times I faced off against Bernard Lagat was at the NCAA Cross Country West Regional Championships at Dell Urich Golf Course in Tucson on Nov. 15, 1997 . . .
(© 1997 Arizona Daily Star)

. . . We were close, but Bernard managed to pull ahead of me for second place.
(University of Arizona Athletics)

Ready to make my move on John Lawson Hill against
Arkansas' Sean Kaley and Adam Goucher (the head behind
Kaley's right shoulder) at the 1998 NCAA Cross Country
Championships at Rim Rock Farm in Lawrence, Kansas.
(Courtesy Abdi Abdirahman)

I proudly became an American on January 28, 2000, in Tucson.
(Courtesy Abdi Abdirahman)

Decked out and enjoying the Sydney Opening Ceremonies with Adam Goucher (left) and Meb Keflezighi (center).
(Courtesy Abdi Abdirahman)

I got to spend time with my U of A teammate and Burundi 800m runner Patrick Nduwimana in the Sydney Olympic Village.
(Courtesy Abdi Abdirahman)

Chasing Meb and Japan's Toshinari Takaoka at Stadium Australia in Sydney. *(Courtesy Abdi Abdirahman)*

Receiving post-race analysis after finishing my first Olympic race. I ran a 28:09.4 to advance to the 10,000m finals.
(Courtesy Abdi Abdirahman)

Duking it out with Meb (left) and
Alan Culpepper (center) at the
2001 USA Outdoor Championships
in Eugene, Oregon. I pulled away for
the win, and all three of us qualified
for the Worlds in Edmonton.
(Courtesy Abdi Abdirahman)

Acknowledging the crowd after my
victory. . . ready for Edmonton.
(Courtesy Abdi Abdirahman)

Coach Murray and me early
in our partnership.
(Courtesy Abdi Abdirahman)

Three silhouettes in front of the Sierra Nevada mountains.
Me, Ryan Shay (center), and Meb (right).
(Courtesy Alicia Vargo)

Hanging out at Pay-N-Take Downtown Market, a popular hangout for
Flagstaff runners, with Jonah Anthony, son of Sean Anthony, the associate
director at the Center for High Altitude Training. Locals threw a party
for me after I qualified for the 2008 Olympic team—including a gift
of a black sombrero for the Black Cactus. *(Courtesy Sean Anthony)*

Posing with U.S. middle distances coach
Ron Mann (left) at a workout in China before
the 2008 Olympics. *(Courtesy Ron Mann)*

The Beijing Opening
Ceremony at the Bird's Nest
was a special night. Here I
am with flag bearer Lopez
Lomong (left) . . .
(Courtesy Ron Mann)

. . . and here I am with the sharp-dressed U.S. distance crew.
(Courtesy Ron Mann)

Midway through the 2012 U.S. Olympic Marathon Team Trials, the lead pack fuels up. *(Photo © Kevin Morris)*

Hanging tough in the final quarter mile for third place and my first Olympic marathon-qualifying performance.
(Photo © Kevin Morris)

Posing in front of a photo of me with Sean Anthony at his office.
Sean is CEO and founder of HYPO2, which helps athletes who
come to Flagstaff for altitude-training camps.
(Courtesy Sean Anthony)

Posing on the streets of New York at a postrace lunch after
the NYC Marathon with other elite runners, including Meb Keflezighi
(second from left), Dathan Ritzenhein (fourth from left), Wesley Korir
(fifth from left), and Yonas Kifle (far right). *(Courtesy Ron Mann)*

Accepting my induction into the Pima Community
College Athletics Hall of Fame in 2013.
(Ray Suarez/Pima Community College)

Returning to where it all began. Visiting my first track coach,
Jim Mielke, at Pima Community College in 2018.
(Pima Community College)

Turning onto Boylston Street near the end of my first Boston Marathon, in 2014. *(Photo © Kevin Morris)*

Chatting with fellow Nike runners Micah Kogo and Stephen Sambu before the 2015 Falmouth Road Race. It was a DNF day for me, but Stephen and Micah went 1-2 in the seven-miler. *(Photo © Kevin Morris)*

Checking out the competition in the 2015 USA 20K Championships in New Haven. I placed sixth. *(Photo © Kevin Morris)*

Diane Nukuri breaking the tape to win the 2015 Falmouth Road Race.
We were just starting to date around this time. *(Photo © Kevin Morris)*

Diane and me, all dressed up in Boston in 2017,
where we both finished top 10 in the marathon.
(Courtesy Diane Nukuri)

Team Mudane: me, Bashir (middle), and Mo (right).
(Courtesy Abdi Abdirahman)

Bashir Abdi says when I run well, I eat good food and tell jokes. I must have had a good workout this day.
(Courtesy Abdi Abdirahman)

Bashir Abdi (left) and me enjoying a tea on a break in Ethiopia.
(Courtesy Abdi Abdirahman)

Jake Riley and me at the moment we knew we were headed to the 2020
Olympics, with Leonard Korir just seconds behind. *(Photo © Kevin Morris)*

Galen Rupp received one of the biggest hugs
I've ever given. *(Photo © Kevin Morris)*

When Team Mudane trains in Sululta, on the outskirts of Addis
Ababa, we have lots of talented runners join us in our warmups and
workouts. This photo was taken in February 2021, when I was getting
in shape for the delayed Tokyo Olympics. *(Photo © Chris Cooper)*

The Black Cactus logo, updated
for 2021. *(Courtesy Abdi Abdirahman)*

Part IV
London 2012

A LESSON
IN HUMILITY

———

"Everything fell apart, from our home in Somalia to Kenya
to the journey to America. It was difficult for us all, but we
went through it. It was a painful time. Abdi was my helper.
We went through a lot together, him and I especially, because
he was my oldest and he was my right hand. I realize he doesn't
like to remember that, and most of the time we just ignore it.
It wasn't a life that we expected."

—Halima Ahmed Handuleh, my mother

10

EMBRACING TRANSITIONS
AND OPPORTUNITIES

After my family arrived in Malindi, Kenya, in 1991, we had no place to go. Thousands of us Somalis were lost once we got off the boat, not knowing what would come next. But my family had our own urgent situation to deal with—keeping my prematurely born sister alive.

Despite the uncertainty, for us kids it seemed a little like an adventure. We were still together and safe. Maybe we could even go home soon. I surely knew better than to believe that, but I wanted to stay positive for my younger siblings. Hearing about the sunken boat we could have been on was initially frightening, but I didn't dwell on it. For my parents, it was a different story. They kept up a united front in looking confident, but they didn't invite questions and we knew better than to ask many.

From what we could tell, Mom and Dad had things under control. But of course they did not. They were taking it day by day. They had six kids, including a newborn now, to take care of in a new country. They didn't know where we were going to stay or what we were going to eat, and anything familiar was 700 miles away in a country in the early stages of tearing itself apart.

Looking back now, I can say we were taking the first steps of a long transition. Two and a half more years would pass before it was complete.

One thing I learned about transitions then is that help from others is what gets you through them. Sometimes you ask for it, and sometimes support falls in your lap, but you're going to need it to see your way through difficult changes. My friend Alicia experienced it from her new community of Flagstaff after her husband, Ryan Shay, died. My friend Lopez Lomong followed the advice of an older boy who told him to join other Lost Boys in escaping captivity where he would have either died or, if he were lucky, stayed alive and become a child soldier. Lopez called the boy his "angel." The Italian woman Giannina was a godsend for us in Malindi when we didn't know where to go. She also helped my parents figure out a long-term solution.

Within a week, doctors in Malindi decided my baby sister needed to be transferred to a hospital in Mombasa, 75 miles (120km) farther down the Indian Ocean coast. Desperate Somalis continued to flow into Kenya, and a refugee camp was being built in Mombasa. My parents' next decision was therefore pretty clear. Mombasa's a major tourism and port city located on an island, but it is big enough that it extends deep into the mainland. Not surprisingly, the refugee camp was located inland. It wasn't scenic beachside property. Small shacks made of wood or corrugated metal housed big families in what looked like a giant fairgrounds parking lot. We had common cooking areas where my mother used beans, flour, and other staples that were distributed throughout the camp.

Mombasa would be our home for the foreseeable future.

$$\mathcal{Z} \; \mathcal{Z} \; \mathcal{Z}$$

That transition from my childhood in Somalia to a Kenyan refugee camp was not the only transition I would face. In 2010, I had reached a crossroads between the spectacle of Beijing and the possibility of London. The 10,000m had given me a lifeline for my third Olympics after the Marathon Trials resulted in a DNF and an emotionally draining day. It is a natural progression for middle-distance runners to take on the marathon full-time as they age, and yet there I was, six years removed from my first 26.2-miler, four years since my marathon PR, still deciding if I should continue running laps around the oval or commit to the roads.

Here's what Jim Gerweck of *Runner's World* said about my 2010 self in an April 12, 2012, article:

> But halfway through the Olympiad, it looked like Abdirahman's career was in its closing act. He seemed to flip-flop between the roads and track, running just 28:35.79 for eighth place at the 2009 U.S. outdoor track championships. "I was all over the place; I didn't have a focus," he admits. "I was struggling with injuries, just kind of going through the motions. I was racing on the track but trying to train for the marathon at the same time."

Plenty of others were questioning my future in the sport too. Running journalists and commenters on message boards figured I was about done. Even conversations with Nike representatives reminded me that I didn't have a lifetime contract with them and changes could be coming.

Mentally, I felt like I was middle-of-the-pack for the first time since I started running, and it happened quickly after such a great stretch in 2007–08. I missed out on the World Track and Field Championships in 2009 and 2011. My New York times and places in the half (1:02:51, fourth) and full marathons (2:14, ninth) in 2009 showed a significant decline—two minutes slower in the half and three minutes slower in the marathon may not sound like much, but at the professional level it's a career killer. In 2010, a year with no Olympics or Worlds, I DNF'd at the New York half in March and didn't race the second half of the year because of a series of injuries that I tried to convince myself were minor but would not go away. My hip was the biggest concern.

I could have tried to argue with reporters, fans, Nike. I could have explained that nagging injuries were making it difficult to run at 100 percent. But could I really blame any of the doubters for thinking I was just about done? I did wonder if retiring was the best decision, but I'm one of those people who, if you tell me I can't do something, I will show you that I can. I didn't like getting on social media, which was becoming pervasive at that time. I never like hearing other people question me. Does anybody want that?

But you can't let that stick in your mind. I look at it like this: there's luck and there's action in life. If you find a $20 bill, that's luck. If you finish on the podium, that's an accomplishment. Sometimes luck works in your favor, and I'm not going to turn down a $20 bill. But you can't rely on luck. You make a decision to do all you can through hard work to achieve your goal.

People are surprised when I say this, but at the end of the day, the negativity didn't bother me for long. In fact, I mostly laughed at it. If you listen to other people who tweet and write that you are done, then you *are* done. I'm a runner, and running is an individual sport. I can't hide behind anybody. I have to do the work to keep doing what I love. I don't like when I'm not running at my best or when I'm injured. Of course that's frustrating. But not because I worry about what they're saying about me. I just don't like it when I'm not in position to reach the podium. I figure everybody is entitled to their opinion, and it's my job to do the work to prove them wrong. I get a kick out of doing that, and hearing doubters only gives me an opportunity to do it.

As for Nike, they had been good to me for over a decade, and it's a business. If I didn't perform well, they would drop me. I always knew that, and also . . . I agreed with it. I wasn't asking for anything for free. I knew the deal: make national teams, get rewarded. Get paid for good results or move on to another job. I didn't take it personally, and I didn't get down about all this talk. Instead, Coach Murray and I got serious. If I wanted to stay in the sport, I needed to make a decision. It was time to face a different kind of transition.

The marathon would be my home for the foreseeable future.

$$\mathcal{Z} \quad \mathcal{Z} \quad \mathcal{Z}$$

I loved running on the track. There is camaraderie on the European Grand Prix circuit, and it was a great way to see some beautiful cities. I like jostling for position and finding gaps between runners to slingshot through at just the right time. The cheering of 90,000 fans in an Olympic stadium is unmatched by any other event I can think of. I got to experience that three times. I don't know if Bono gets bored singing "I Still Haven't Found What I'm Looking For" to a packed arena after thousands of concerts, but I don't think I would.

Still, I wanted to continue running professionally, and it was pretty clear to Coach Murray and me that bumping up the distance to the half marathon, marathon, and other road races—15Ks, 20Ks—was the way for me to do that. It was a natural progression that many runners had followed as they got older and (I hope) smarter. My final race on the track was June 23, 2011, at the U.S. Championships at historic Hayward Field in Eugene— speaking of incredible places to run that I knew I was going to miss. I placed 15th in the 10,000m in a disappointing time of 28:57.79, not nearly good enough to make the U.S. team going to the World Championships. I steered clear of the steeplechase water jump; no celebration after that one.

CHASING ABDI

From Go Be More podcast with Bryan Green and Jon Rankin, episode 28, July 17, 2020.

Me: I love running. For me, that's my peaceful place where I process everything, if I'm feeling something, if I'm not doing well. At the end of the day, we go through roller coasters, especially the past few months. For me, the best place I feel safe is to go drive somewhere and just go for a jog—not even a run. Just jog, sweat. Put on a jacket, put your shoes on, no one is there, no music, nothing. Just find a couple-mile loop, just do that loop. I finish that couple miles, man, I feel just rejuvenated, 100 percent refreshed. That gives me peace of mind. That's my medication. That's my addiction. Man, I just love it.

Jon: When you have success, you put pressure on yourself, and that love can get lost. How have you been able to hold onto the love and keep being successful?

Me: Success doesn't come overnight. It takes time, dedication, sacrifice to get where you are in life. There's also a humbleness involved. When you get where you want to get and have success, people are going to look up to you. When that happens, is that success going to change you, or are you going to be the same person and do the same things that got you there. My key words have always been to be humble, be a gracious winner, and also be a gracious loser. It doesn't matter how successful you've become, treat others the way you want to be treated. That was my secret. I try not to let the success get over to my head or think I'm better than other runners. Just be who I am. Just surround yourself with the same people who have been with you from day one. Keep the same friends. That's simple for me. That's the only way I can explain it, to be honest.

Bryan: You've got the internal pressure you put on yourself, but you've also got the external pressure of coaching staff and trainers. You've got sponsors and other people who are investing in your career. If you get down, you can't let that spiral. You have to find a way to step back and have perspective. . . . You can have a thousand great races and a bad race and it's easy to think about the bad race.

Me: Exactly. It's the first thing that comes to mind in the heat of the moment. I'm not saying I don't feel like that when I don't do well, when I drop a race. It hurts and it's just the worst thing for an athlete when you get that feeling. But it's how you bounce back. That's when your coaching or your friends or your loved ones come. You have to have a good support system. You don't get to the top of the mountain by yourself. There's always those people behind you, your family members, your friends, your coaches. No one sees those people. They only see you, and the glamor, the interviews, the good life. But they don't see the sacrifice that your loved ones make.

A big part of why transitions are important is that they are, by definition, a move from what has been to what will be. And once you accept that reality, you can clear your mind of a lot of confusion and fear. Letting go of the past can be hard because there is comfort there—even if it includes bad experiences—and the future is, also by definition, uncertain. But if you see that what is in the past isn't helping you create what you want in the days ahead, letting go is exactly what you must do. My success would now be determined in a relatively few races each year on the roads. That was a little scary, but I put my transition into perspective. If my parents hadn't been willing to act after seeing the bigger picture of what was happening in Somalia, I don't even want to think about what would have happened to us. My siblings and I would certainly not have been able to achieve what we have.

Thanks to my dad, Mohammed, and mom, Halima, we have all been able to do impressive things. I get asked all types of questions because I'm a pro runner: What is your training like? What exactly was going through your head on the 21st lap? What do I think about <insert another runner's name here> changing coaches? What was it like growing up in Africa? What will you do when you retire from the sport? What is your view on <insert U.S. government's foreign policy initiative here>? What is your view on <insert late-breaking news of the world here>? But my parents and my brothers and sisters have views on many of these issues that are just as thoughtful as mine. Well, maybe not what I was thinking about in the middle of a race, but do we really need to scrutinize such things so much, anyway? Maybe more often our instinct should be to ask intelligent people who aren't famous for their suggestions on how to make the world a better place.

I think my six younger siblings all have lived amazing lives. Because I'm the oldest and they moved to Seattle shortly after I started at the University of Arizona, sometimes I feel like my experience in Africa and the United States has been very different from theirs. I don't talk about them publicly very often because people don't ask much about my family, and my family doesn't seek out the spotlight anyway. But each is successful in their own way, and I'm proud of all of them. Three of my sisters are nurses and care for people as my family was cared for in Malindi and Mombasa.

My brother Ayanle is the second oldest. He was a software developer at Microsoft, then left to help start another company, all before he turned 40. Professional sports are weird that way: in practically every other profession, people strive to retire early and are congratulated when they do. But aging athletes get asked when they're going to quit, as if they need to exit the stage for others to get a chance. Those who hang on the longest are praised, but only if they don't perform poorly on their way out the door.

Ayanle ran the 400m and 800m in high school. His times were really good, and by then I had been to the 2000 Olympics, so coaches recruited him pretty heavily. You're going to be better than your brother, everyone said. But he didn't want that kind of pressure. He joined ROTC in college and within a year, he was in one of the first Army units to invade Iraq in 2003.

I love my family in part because they are very practical people. None of them has ever been to an Olympics or even to see me in a professional track or road race. I think Ayanle saw me run a couple times in college. My parents went to a college meet in Tucson once. Their reasoning is simple: it's expensive to travel, and we'd rather watch you on TV. At a marathon, we'd only get to see you pass by us one time, they say. They simply congratulate me when I do well and say "better luck next time" when I don't.

I think culture plays a part in their approach. School activities are not a big deal in Somalia. School is, and I got good marks in math, which made them proud. When I was in high school, they were adapting to a new country. So was I. I was already out of the house before I started running, so they didn't have to drive me to and from track meets. My parents supported my choice to become a runner, just as they supported all of their children's job choices. That's all I need.

Whether I make the Olympics or DNF, they love me. Whether we agree or disagree on issues of the world, they love me and I love them. I've never doubted that, and I certainly didn't doubt it in 2011 when I was transitioning to the marathon. If I was frustrated or injured, I could call my mom and we'd talk about anything but running. I gain strength and perspective by being around people who are determined to persevere—and for me, that starts with family.

$$\mathcal{F} \quad \mathcal{F} \quad \mathcal{F}$$

I have never been one to drastically change my training routine. But I no longer was serving two masters—the 10,000m and the marathon. I realized I needed to do more long stuff and less of the balls-to-the-wall speedwork that I loved to do with Bernard Lagat and others. I'm pretty sure my body was reacting to the fits and starts of marathon training with injuries in 2010 and 2011. When I finally committed fully to the marathon, I really internalized for the first time the idea that I didn't always have to redline workouts. Coach Murray gradually pushed up my mileage to 120 miles per week. I could handle the additional hours on my feet. In fact, I enjoyed the freedom of having a clear purpose again.

I was 34 years old after the 2011 U.S. Championships, and I could finally admit to myself with no regrets that the second half of my career was just beginning. The U.S. Olympic Marathon Trials were just seven months away. It was time to get to work.

11

ANSWERING DOUBTERS
IN HOUSTON

The most uncertain time of my career was when I stood in chilly downtown Houston, Texas, on January 14, 2012, for the U.S. Olympic Marathon Trials.

My fitness and training weren't the problem. I even had some proof that concentrated marathon training was making a difference when I won the U.S. 20K Championships in New Haven, Connecticut, four months earlier. As the Trials approached, Coach Murray lowered my 120-mile weeks to around 100 miles a week but with my longest tempo runs coming in at the full or nearly full marathon distance, something I had never done in training before. Believe it or not, even though I had finished five marathons, I had never run farther in a workout than 20 miles before I began preparing for the Houston Trials.

The uncertainty came from the fact that I hadn't run a marathon since 2009, and I hadn't been tested in one since I had acknowledged to myself I wouldn't be racing on the track anymore. I was all in, and if it didn't go to plan, then . . . well, what exactly was my future in the sport? The questions came from all over—fans, media, sponsors. To them, I had been dealing with injuries and inconsistent performances for three years. I was getting the obituary treatment. You know what that is, right? When people talk about you with kind words but as though you are already gone: "Oh, Abdi. He had a good run as a pro," or "That Abdi sure did accomplish a lot in his time."

Since I was only on roads now, I didn't have as many opportunities to forget a bad race. And a bad race in the Olympic Trials is definitely not going to quiet the doubters.

I didn't feel that way myself. At all. But there are no guarantees. There are never any guarantees. I was in good shape in Houston. To listen to commentators leading up to the Trials, you would think Meb and Ryan Hall were the only ones in the race. But if no one else saw me as a threat, I sure did. I still felt like I was getting acclimated to marathons, and I did my best to stop listening to the distractions. It wasn't always easy, to be honest. I may be pretty chill most of the time, but I am as competitive as anybody you will meet. When it's a big race, I show up and compete. So as I made my way to the starting area in Houston, my agent, Ray Flynn, wished me luck. I told him I would make the team. I meant it and he knew it. All the other distractions washed away as I stood beside Meb, Ryan, and the other prerace favorites on the front line of a field with 111 men vying for three spots.

CHASING ABDI

"My first impression of Abdi was his carefree attitude and his love for life. Wherever you see him, it's palpable. I didn't travel internationally with him a lot, but I was at major marathons with him and we'd hang out in the hospitality rooms. Abdi would come over and have breakfast with [2012 Boston Marathon winner] Wesley Korir and me. Abdi has a great sense of humor, but you don't realize how deep he is. He has a philosophical base about him if you start talking to him about his ideas and life in general. If you're Abdi's friend, you're a friend for life."

—Ron Mann, U.S. men's coach, 2005 World Championships
team, 2008 Olympic middle distances

American distance-running legend Frank Shorter shot the starter's pistol, and we were off. Already at 10 miles it was a five-man race, with Meb, Ryan, Dathan Ritzenhein, first-time marathoner Mo Trafeh, and me. Everyone knew Ryan wanted to push the pace, but I, too, wanted everybody else to chase us. I felt great, and I was putting in mini-surges every now and then to see who wanted to come along.

Just under halfway, after I tried out one of these, NBC announcer Craig Masback said this about me: "He's a bit of a mystery man in the marathon, better known as a 10,000-meter runner. He's run a 2:08:56 in the marathon, one of the best times of this group up in the front here. But he's been inconsistent in the marathon, and frankly no one was sure what to expect from him. When we saw him the other day, he said he's fit. He always has a smile on his face, always is confident, so you're never quite sure how to take that."

His broadcast partner, two-time Olympian Todd Williams, agreed that I was flying under the radar and said I had great credentials from the 5000 and 10,000m: "He looks extremely smooth and relaxed."

It's true. I was chatting with Ryan and even smiling a little bit. When I'm clicking in a race or workout, I talk. In workouts, I might tease the others and see if I can get under their skin to entertain myself and lighten the mood. But in races, I encourage the guys around me to work together so we all benefit. At 15 miles, we dropped Trafeh. At mile 18, we dropped Ritz, who had placed ninth in the marathon at Beijing, one place ahead of Ryan. They had fallen away quickly, and the fact that Ritz hadn't responded well was my signal that this was a great opportunity for me.

Still, I knew a top-three spot was not secure yet. I had expended a lot of energy pushing the pace, and my two friends and competitors looked hungry. We knew we had an advantage over Ritz, since we had the three of us to help each other along. It was like three against one. But we also understood that in the final two miles, we would be in it for ourselves.

With three miles to go, Meb powered ahead and Ryan followed, their spots to London pretty clearly in the bag. I fell back and was only leading Ritz by about 25 seconds. I focused on just staying as close to five-minute pace as I could, figuring that for all I knew, Ritz might be struggling as much as I was, and with even farther to go. The downtown loop course had turns pretty much every 400 or 800 meters, so I could keep my eye on how much of a lead I had on him. But that 25th mile was brutal. The finish line could not arrive soon enough for me, and every city block I put behind me didn't seem to be getting me any closer to it. Finally, I made my last left turn onto Avenida de las Americas. The end was in sight, and it felt like the happiest sight of my life. I caught a glimpse over my left shoulder that Ritz was gaining from behind, but knowing I was that close gave me the boost I needed to hold him off by eight seconds.

When I crossed the finish line, I threw my arms in the air and found Meb and Ryan for hugs. Meb held his baby daughter Yohana in his arms, and soon all four of us were embracing in a big circle draped by a giant American flag.

I remember many of my races clearly in my mind, as do a lot of runners. But that one was special. I know how badly I was hurting and that Ritz might have gotten me if he had another half mile. I know how hard I had worked to put myself in position to make my fourth Olympic team, this time in a new event under a lot of question marks about my ability. I thought back to how differently we all felt today compared to the tragic Trials four years earlier in Central Park. Three of my good friends and I had all run under 2:10, the first time that had happened at a U.S. Olympic Trials.

It had been a long time, but for a moment I felt there were no doubters, no negative energies around me.

That optimism was short-lived, however. I hadn't even left the George R. Brown Convention Center before I was stunned by news that was breaking while we were racing. I was walking down the convention center hallway when a LetsRun.com reporter asked me about the race. He asked about my training with the "Arizona guys" in the weeks leading up to the Trials and mentioned Stephen Sambu, a good friend and nine-time All-American at the University of Arizona. I said that I run with those guys most of the time—"those guys" also including U of A national cross country champion Lawi Lalang, his brother Boaz Lalang, Aussie David McNeill from Northern Arizona University, and Mexican Olympian Juan Luis Barrios—but before Houston, Ezkyas Sisay, an Ethiopian who placed a surprising ninth at New York City two months earlier, had been helping me on tempo runs and long runs.

"You were doing some training with Martin Fagan, right?" the reporter asked me.

"Yes, I was training with Martin too. He got hurt and just left. Martin is a great guy and in such good shape but I kind of feel bad for him," I replied. "If he stays healthy . . ."

I didn't get a chance to finish my thought.

"Yeah, but you heard about him testing positive yesterday?"

I was stunned and stopped walking. "What happened?"

"He tested positive for EPO. Oh, I thought you knew."

My eyes got huge. I didn't know what to say. I had no idea.

"They asked me to ask Abdi about it, if he saw anything or knew anything," he said.

"Oh man, I didn't know anything," I said.

"Supposedly it's the first test. I guess Keith Kelly was coaching him a little bit, and Keith said he admitted it to him."

"It's crazy," I said as I started walking again. "That's the first thing I heard right now. He was staying in my house. I didn't see anything. And one day he was running with me and he said, oh, I run too hard for him and he left."

"Oh, quickly, like in the middle of a training session?" the reporter asked.

"Yeah, in the middle of a training session," I continued. "We were running in the middle of a training session. I live in a gated community. It's a mile and a half to my gate. On Sunday we were gonna go for a long run but when we got to 400 meters he said 'Hey, I don't feel good, man, I'm gonna leave.'"

"Was that recently?"

"Yeah, that was just a couple weeks ago."

"He was just hurting and you never saw him again?"

"I never saw him again. He just left and went back to Flagstaff and then I heard he went back to Ireland. I didn't know what was going on. He said he was hurting and didn't want to run anymore."

"It makes sense now. He must have known or something."

"I don't know," I said. "It's kind of a sad situation but at the same time it's real bad news for the sport. I'm kind of disappointed with him because I like to associate with people who are clean. . . . It's bad news, actually. I'm real disappointed for him, as a person."

Doping is a perpetual issue that threatens the integrity of track and field. If some runners cheat and get an unfair advantage, it makes it hard for fans of the sport to believe in the best thing about it: the joy and challenge of watching human athletic performance at its highest level. I have always been clear about my position on the matter. I sleep well at night because I know all that I have accomplished has been done without any illegal substances or methods. No way would I continue to run if I had to break the rules or jeopardize my body to do well.

I bought a wall hanging at Bed Bath & Beyond back in 2004. I still remember it because I was getting ready for the Athens Olympics. I have it in my bedroom in Tucson. It reads: "Follow the path of your destiny with purpose and open heart." I keep it up because it reminds me to make decisions that help me control my own results as best as I can, and to do so with integrity and openness to the rest of the world. It's a simple message that keeps me focused—it even reminds me of the football team's quote from the *Friday Night Lights* TV series when they get ready for the game: "Clear eyes, full hearts, can't lose." Life becomes complicated when people crave success they see in others, and that can lead to those people making poor decisions.

Martin later said depression and thoughts of suicide led to EPO use and that he was tested the day after he used it for the first time. I take him at his word; it's not my job to be his jury. If all that is true, I just wish he would have sought help from me or somebody. LetsRun.com interviewed me a few weeks later. Martin had apologized to me by email by then, and through Ray Flynn, the great Irish miler who was our mutual agent.

"At least he admitted he did something wrong and he came clean with it," I told LetsRun.com. "There are people in this world who have done worse than he did. I'm sad for him. He ruined his name and reputation. He wrote me and he was sincerely sorry. . . . I accept his apology as a man. . . . I feel sorry for him as a person.

"This is just running. You have a life to live. We're runners. That's what we do, but we're more than runners. . . . Running is going to come to an end . . . for everybody."

As it turned out, Sisay also tested positive for EPO and received a two-year ban that May. He had to vacate his New York City Marathon place and prize money from the year before, as well as another half-marathon win.

These shameful stories tarnish the good name of the majority of pro runners. I felt like people thought I was guilty by association. Even on the day of the Trials, when I was happy—thrilled beyond belief at my race—I was answering questions about another runner's choices.

That summer, running journalist Erin Strout asked me about Fagan and Sisay in an ESPN article. I told her I had no knowledge of their drug use when we were training.

"I needed somebody to pace my workouts last winter, so I asked Ezkyas to pace two of my tempo runs. He killed me. He kicked my ass," I said. "I work so hard for what I have, then two guys I ran with a couple of times did something wrong and suddenly I'm part of it. I'm glad they got caught—if you cheat, you should be banned for life."

This is the tension I think all of us human beings have—I expressed concern for my running partners, and I also wanted the book thrown at them. Which is it? We want to believe people always do the right things. When they do the wrong things, we want to shun them and not acknowledge they are flawed. I feel strongly that a drug cheat doesn't deserve a second chance. They harm the integrity of the whole sport when they think they can get away with it. But it doesn't mean I ever have to hate the guy.

So which is it?

Both. I want to show compassion, and I also want people to face consequences for their actions.

I have two goals: I want to surround myself with supportive people who care about me as a person and whom I care about. I also want to treat anybody I meet with respect and compassion, knowing that we all have common fears and desires. Most of the time I think I do both of those. We're all doing the best that we can.

In that interview in Houston, I called both of them "great guys," and I meant it. They worked hard and were fun to hang out with. But what they did hurts the sport, themselves, and others who trust them. I would like to say I was more careful about who I trained with after that, but I never thought that I *wasn't* being careful. We just can't know everything that is going on in other people's hearts.

12

ME BEING ME

On my last long, hard run in Tucson before the 2012 Olympic Marathon Trials, I parked my Denali at a trailhead. Twenty miles later, I came back and it was gone. I had run so hard that I thought maybe I was getting light-headed and forgot where I left it. It wasn't too long before I came to my senses and realized my SUV had been stolen. I was able to call James Li to come and pick me up.

I hated losing that vehicle. I bought it soon after signing with Nike, to replace a beat-up 1980 Buick LeSabre I'd been driving. I decided to go another direction when it came time to replace it. In 2011, the BMW Group had signed on as an official partner of the U.S. Olympic Committee and several national governing bodies, including USA Track & Field. As part of that sponsorship, they gave athletes a decent deal on a car, so I took advantage of it and gave myself a BMW. Remember how in *Running with the Buffaloes*, Chris Lear described Adam Goucher as an "American SUV" and me as a "sleek two-door roadster" at the 1998 NCAA cross country meet? Now I could lay claim to having owned both.

That BMW ended up being a nice gift to myself for making the Olympic team. Like my 2004 email address, that car is a daily reminder to me of what it means to be an Olympian. I love driving it down the interstates between Tucson and Flagstaff (though it looks a little more out of place in sleepy-mountain-town Flag).

☞ ☞ ☞

Alicia Vargo says I have "champagne tastes," and I suppose she's right. Anthony Famiglietti says that the way I approach running, I'm not in it for the money, but I like flashy, soft shirts and comfortable, expensive cars because that's my reward to myself for the pain I put myself through. Maybe he's right too.

I don't get a lot of chances to dress up, but in March 2012 I wore a sharp-fitting navy-blue suit at the 20th annual Endurance Live Awards Gala. The event honors endurance athletes across a number of sports, and there I was at the Nokia Theatre in Los Angeles getting my photo taken with Meb and Jenny Simpson, who won a gold medal in the 1500m at the World Championships in Daegu, South Korea, the year before.

One week later, I was inducted into the Road Runners Club of America Distance Running Hall of Fame at a ceremony in Memphis, Tennessee. My fellow inductees were Coach Joe Vigil, then in his 80s, and Linda Somers Smith, a 1996 Olympic marathoner who had continued to race in the open category well after she reached the master's age of 40—all while maintaining an active law practice. At age 50, she had even run at the 2012 Trials in Houston. That Hall of Fame ceremony was one day where I could certainly lay claim to being the young guy in the room. It was an honor to enter the RRCA Hall of Fame with both of them. Wouldn't it be fun to still be running as an elite as long as Linda did?

People were talking about me again that spring and summer, and most of the time—the drug revelations about my two short-term training partners aside—it felt pretty good. I was a comeback story after overcoming a variety of injuries to make the Olympic team. One of those injuries was a stress reaction in my right femur that fortunately never became a full fracture. Though Meb and Ryan got the headlines based on past

140

medals and American records, I was still recognized as one of America's three marathoners with potential to maybe even sneak in and grab a medal on the flat London course, rather than as someone who needed to retire and take up golf.

Golf. That's one luxury activity I don't have any interest in. Can you imagine me playing? When I first started getting a steady income from Nike and Kip Lagat moved to Tucson, we decided on our rest days we should play golf at the country club. We'd deck ourselves out in nice clothes and buy high-end equipment. We were *set*, man! Anybody can run, we told ourselves, but not everybody can golf. We decided we would be high society by being on the golf course. Only . . . I hated it. I loved driving that little cart around. I felt like a kid. Otherwise, I shanked everything. I had no clue where the ball was going when I hit it.

I tried golf again when I was rehabbing my leg in 2011, and it was as boring as I remembered. I'm the slowest walker in the world—I've been told I've run so many miles that I've forgotten how to walk! Still, I might be a *little* faster than Ryan Hall. We once got laughed at a couple of nights before a race in Europe. Our group kept getting far ahead of us as we ambled along after dinner out. Here we were, two guys who can run 26 miles at five-minute pace, but we couldn't keep up with our friends on a leisurely walk. Anyway, after walking the first hole of the golf course, I was tired and ready to go get a burger.

Trying golf taught me a lesson, though. I can easily get excited at the idea of doing something new or buying something flashy, but you have to love it to keep going back to it. I decided once that I would get into photography. It seemed like something I would like, capturing a beautiful moment in time, whether it was a product for sale or a stunning landscape. But I didn't have the patience for it, so my photography career didn't last long.

I definitely like nice things, and I have no problem spending money I've worked hard to earn. But there's no *should*. I like Italian shoes; I hate golf. Maybe for you it's the opposite.

CHASING ABDI

Excerpt from "Brief Chat: Abdirahman and Lagat," an article by Peter Gambaccini in *Runner's World*, April 4, 2012.

Abdirahman and Lagat . . . spoke to reporters by teleconference, joined by New York Road Runners President and CEO Mary Wittenberg.

Peter: Tell us about the first time that you guys spent some time together, maybe even away from running, and what your recollections of that were?

Bernard Lagat: It's been a long time. I think I remember it was '97, and it was great meeting Abdi all the time during NCAAs. And even when I moved into Tucson, part of the main decision making was that even though Coach [James] Li was going into Tucson, I knew my best friend was going to be in Tucson. When I was looking into [buying] the house, Abdi took me around, showing me places, even introducing me to the Realtor that ended up helping me buy a house. So Abdi has been part of my life as a runner and also as a person. After Gladys [Lagat's wife] had Miika and Gianna, Abdi has been like my older son. When he is with Miika and Gianna, you can't differentiate who is a kid and who is an older one. So Abdi has been always a good uncle and almost like a son to me. It's weird to say, but that is Abdi.

Mary Wittenberg: Abdi, what you may not know is whenever it's time to recruit you to a major event, especially around the marathon, we're always checking to see if you're running with Bernard or not because you've had some pretty strong performances when you two are hitting it together.

Me: Definitely that's true, Mary. Bernard always keeps me on my toes. I'm also glad, too, because Bernard always tells me how it is. Gladys always, when she senses that something is not going right, she says, "Abdi, you need to tell me what's going on, you're not training the way you're supposed to be training. What's going on?" The last couple years I've been struggling with injury, like a year and a half, and Gladys knew that, and she would say, "Abdi, just get healthy and everything will be all right." That's kind of the people you want to surround yourself with, but now it's Coach Li, Coach Murray, Gladys, the whole community there has been supportive of me. I wish I could say I make the team by myself, but it's Gladys and the people and Coach Li and Coach Murray, they are a big part of the team. You don't see them, but they're the people who do all the work in the background. I just do the running.

$$\mathcal{Z} \quad \mathcal{Z} \quad \mathcal{Z}$$

I even worked things out with Nike. I had an opportunity to go to another shoe company, but I like to stay with people who believed in me before they had reason to do so. They respected my decision years ago to stay in Arizona when they invited me to train in Oregon, and I never forgot that.

Best of all, I wasn't hearing so much about age (for the record, Meb is almost two years *older* than me). When I did, it was about how I was only the second four-time Olympian among American distance runners. The other was another U of A alumnus, George Young, who competed from 1960–72 and won a bronze medal in the steeplechase in 1968. My longtime Tucson training partner Bernard Lagat has been in five total Olympics, but his first two were as a Kenyan.

Ah, age. This seems to be everybody's fallback reason when things aren't going well in sports. I've been compared to baseball player Manny Ramirez from time to time. He's considered an ageless enigma by some, capable of frustrating performances and odd decisions while also being the force behind some of the greatest hitting displays you'll ever see. He last played a major-league game in 2010 at the age of 38, but for another decade, he bounced around the minor leagues and other countries as a player-coach. The phrase people use when describing the strange things he does is, "That's just Manny being Manny." That 2012 *Runner's World* article by Jim Gerweck asked questions about my ability to still run at a high level, but it was actually a positive article focusing on my return to the Olympics. It was even titled, "Abdi Being Abdi," and he made the comparison this way:

> "There are a lot of people out there on message boards and stuff who don't know what the hell they're talking about," Abdirahman says. "But that's OK, we need them; they motivate us to get out and train to prove them wrong. Coming into the trials people doubted me; they were saying, This guy is done, he should retire. When I'm done, I'll know I'm done. I'll walk off the track—you won't have to push me off. . . ."

> Through a long and often stellar career, Abdirahman has had moments that make the casual observer question his focus and dedication, or at the very least, his attention to the small details of his sport. Like surging into the lead midway through a national championship road race—and right off course, missing a key turn and going from first to fifth in the space of three strides. Or failing to wear a hat or long sleeves in a single-digit temperature cross country championship—not the wisest tactic for a rail-thin East African emigre with a shaved head—and succumbing to the cold halfway through the race.

> Those who know him well, however, say, to crib a phrase often applied to Manny Ramirez, another supremely gifted athlete with fluctuating focus, that's just "Abdi being Abdi." For every athletic racing gaffe or sub-par, seemingly half-hearted performance, there have been 10 efforts of sheer brilliance, dotted with multiple national titles and near American records. Through it all, Abdirahman has faced races, and life in general, with a laid-back, *que sera, sera* outlook that seems the antithesis of the highly focused, driven attitude displayed by most distance runners of his pedigree.

"That's just the way I am, always have been," he says. "I'm just laid back, enjoying life. You can't be going 100 percent all the time, every day—you need to back off, physically and mentally, or you won't last. I think that's the reason I've had such a long career.

"I know what races count, and if you look at my career, when it came to that point I was usually ready. No one remembers how fast you ran in early season races, but they never forget how many national championships you won or Olympic teams you made."

All I can do is laugh at my ups and downs. I was struggling in 2011, then reeled off a dominating win at the U.S. 20K Championships in New Haven, Connecticut, with a time of 1:00:12 on September 5. Hey, that's why we run the race rather than just give the victory to the favorite. To be honest, I'm not sure what races he was referring to. I've taken a wrong turn a few times. I get locked into the moment and forget to look up. And it was really cold at the 2004 national cross country championships, but I took fifth there and qualified for the world meet. Anyway, I think these examples overshadow how helpful it is for me not to get overly anxious about the details of life. I'd be wound really tight if I never allowed myself to eat some greasy foods or if I forced myself to run 10 miles on a day when my body needed rest. Almost from the beginning of our relationship, Coach Murray has given me permission to tell him I am taking the day off. I rarely use it, and he knows I don't take advantage of it. If I do use it, it's because I know it is best for my body. Also, I know how hard I work to get ready for the big races—they're the reason I want to run. If I'm remembered for those, I'll be happy.

A comparison I prefer is with quarterback Tom Brady. I've never met him, but he definitely seems intense and obsessive about every variable. That's not me. However, nobody will ever say he didn't work hard or wasn't competitive, and that *is* me. He's 4 1/2 months younger than me, and I know his background very well, how he was a sixth-round pick—199th overall—when he came out of the University of Michigan. He came to prominence early in the new century by winning his first Super Bowl in 2002, just a few months after I made my fourth national team. He tore his ACL in the first game of 2008—three weeks after the Beijing Olympics—and missed the entire season. He lost Super Bowl XLVI a month after the 2012 Olympic Trials.

Like me, he's experienced the podium and the DNF. Like me in mid-career, he was still doing impressive things, but football commentators were beginning to ask how long he could keep going, just like the track world questioned me. In fact, he led the Tampa Bay Buccaneers to a championship in 2021 at age 43. The week before Super Bowl LV, Brady said he wants to play when he's 45 years old or even longer:

> I think I'll know when it's time. I don't know when that time will come. But I think I'll know. And I'll understand that I gave everything I could give to this game. You put a lot into it. I don't think I could ever go at this game half-ass. I've gotta put everything into it. When I put it all out there, [when] I feel like I can't do it anymore, I don't feel like I can commit to the team in the way that the team needs me, then I think that's when it's probably time to walk away.

That's how I feel about my career.

I look at him as a contemporary, an example of what you can do if you take care of yourself and don't settle for second best. He could have retired after a couple of Super Bowls. Why does he come back? He has everything you could ever want in life. We have very different personalities, but when it comes to what counts in our athletic lives, we're two sides of the same coin. He loves his sport. So do I. He's motivated to keep coming back. So am I.

Am I Manny Ramirez? Am I Tom Brady? At the end of the day, I'm Abdi, and I'm proud of what I've accomplished and how I've done it.

$$\tilde{\jmath} \quad \tilde{\jmath} \quad \tilde{\jmath}$$

After so much doubt for so long, London was actually shaping up to be something special. I was feeling fast, having not spent much time in

Flagstaff that year. People talk about altitude training as this automatic advantage, but it takes a toll on the body too. Coach Murray and I believed that since my fitness was finally consistently strong, I would be better off with more extended tempo runs like what I did before the Trials. Tempo runs allowed my legs to churn faster and faster underneath me, and at high elevation there is a limit to how long you can push the body at that intensity. The flat course in London was well suited to my emphasis that year on building speed.

Less than two months out, I won my ninth national title at the U.S. Half Marathon Championships in Duluth, Minnesota. I forced the field of 99 men to chase me from the start with a 4:37 mile. Brett Gotcher stayed close. Ten miles in, Ian Burrell joined us and took a brief lead. He actually did us a favor because Brett and I, who knew each other well from training in Flagstaff, were starting to slow. We answered the call and dropped Ian, then I surged at the 11-mile mark and held off Brett for the final two miles for a three-second win: 1:02:46.

Soon after that victory, my right knee started hurting during my final buildup to the Olympics. It was painful, but not so much that I couldn't keep running. Still, you have to listen to your body, and the persistent throbbing was definitely a concern. U.S. Olympic Committee doctors said I had water on my knee, but it wasn't excessive and I should be fine. I arrived in London in time for the Opening Ceremonies confident that with the tapering period to rest, I was still in position to have one of my best marathons.

CHASING ABDI

This week on "Holla Atcha Boy!," my man. I call him "Abi-runnin," but his real name is Abdi Abirahman . . . Abdirahman.

—Jamie Nieto, Olympic high jumper, on his "Holla Atcha Boy!" online web series episode, after the 2012 Olympics

Quickly it became clear that was wishful thinking. My knee was hurting, and on a course with short stretches of cobblestone, 107 turns, and four U-turns it was especially brutal. I rarely DNF, but I didn't want to do long-term damage. I made the sensible decision. Shortly after passing Buckingham Palace and the start/finish area for the second time on the loop course, I ended my first Olympic marathon, around mile 11. Ryan Hall had been dealing with a hamstring issue and shut down just a couple minutes before me. This was not the triple-threat American showing that we had hoped for. But Meb ran a fantastic race that day and barely missed the podium, with a fourth-place finish.

I was so happy for Meb. After he missed the 2008 Olympics, he came back with a showing almost as impressive as his silver medal from 2004. But to be honest, on a selfish level this race stuck with me longer than most. Even now, sometimes I'll finish a training run or be daydreaming at my house, and I wonder what I could have done that day if everything had gone well. I remember how fit I was. I was doing the best workouts of my life. I did a 12x1km in 2:45 with a one-minute jog recovery. A few weeks before that, I did a 20-mile progression run, starting with 5:10s and getting down to 4:40s the last couple miles. Even though I pride myself on being able to recover from a bad day—you have to move on from disappointment in life or you'll drive yourself crazy—I'd be lying if I said I didn't play the "What if" game with myself when I think of London 2012. My workouts didn't pay off. I had an opportunity to do something special, and it just didn't happen.

Dropping out was the hardest thing to do, yet I knew pushing too hard could create bigger problems. I left London disappointed, but I returned to Tucson and spent time with my friends who didn't care how I did. I ran the U.S. 10-Mile Road Running Championships in St. Paul, Minnesota, that fall to test out my knee. I placed 13th in 48:12 and felt confident that I could take some time off and begin the 2013 season healthy.

Regarding my high-end cars, I want to clarify something. I've had that BMW for nine years and counting. I had the Denali for 10. I take care of what I have, including my body. After all that had happened over the past few years, one thing I knew for sure after London was that, like my cars, my body wasn't going to retire anytime soon.

London

I had been to the capital of the United Kingdom four times before the 2012 Olympics, but always to compete in the London Athletics Grand Prix meet on the European track circuit. It was held at the National Sports Centre at Crystal Palace, a beautiful old stadium in the south part of the city. Competing in the marathon, which meant tracing the paths past and around historic and cultural sites such as Big Ben, Trafalgar Square, and the Tower of London, felt just as intimate. At the National Sports Centre, spectators felt right on top of you, the way an athletics venue should be. Along the streets of London, fans cheered us on virtually every step of the way, practically right on top of us as well.

The marathon received additional attention that year because of Guor Marial, a runner born in Sudan who had attended college at Iowa State University. Guor had lost dozens of his family to the civil war in Sudan, which had led to the creation of the newest country on the planet, South Sudan. Having just gained its independence one year earlier, South Sudan was still struggling to get on its feet. Understandably, it had not yet formed a functioning national Olympic committee. This put Guor in limbo. He refused to run for Sudan because the government had brutalized his family and friends. But South Sudan wasn't yet prepared to field an Olympic team. The International Olympic Committee's rules meant he couldn't run if he wasn't representing an IOC member nation.

Under a lot of international pressure, the IOC gave him permission to compete under the Olympic banner. Guor became known as the runner without a country. At the Opening Ceremonies—Coach Murray always tells me not to, but I go every time!—he entered the Stadium at Queen Elizabeth Olympic Park by himself, carrying a flag with the familiar five Olympic rings. The sold-out crowd cheered wildly for him, even more than they did for athletes from many other countries.

The concept of being a runner without a country really made an impression on me. I thought of Kip Lagat, who, like me, was competing in his fourth Olympics. He had represented Kenya and America. I thought of Meb and me, both representing America again after having been fortunate enough to survive the conflicts in our home countries. And Lopez Lomong, now an American Olympian for a second time, had escaped Sudan. No one ever told us we couldn't run just because we came to a new country.

Guor was gracious in interviews before and during the London Games and used the media attention to alert people to the devastation in Sudan. I gain some measure of hope when I see these opportunities arise—when sporting events allow athletes to share their stories that teach people about the broader world. It's a complicated question as to whether sports can change the world, but on an individual level, each of us absolutely can make a difference. I've seen it many times just in my life as a distance runner, thanks to friends of mine like Kip, Guor, Lopez, Meb, and many others. Slowly . . . very slowly . . . I was starting to realize it might be good for me to go back to the continent where my story began.

Part V
Rio de Janeiro 2016

A LESSON
IN PERSEVERANCE

———

"Abdi, you're like an American on the inside but you
look like an African on the outside."

—Bashir Abdi, my friend and training partner

13

REJUVENATED
IN ARIZONA

Trails in Tucson get me daydreaming. I know I'm supposed to focus, but sometimes the best part of running is the opportunity to lose myself in my thoughts.

When I'm in the rolling hills of Saguaro National Park–West, I love the 4 1/2-mile "Abdi Loop" (as Kip Lagat calls it) because I would be able to punish him on it, payback for what he does to me on the track. Kip and I have covered the Rillito River Path, Huckleberry Loop, and dozens more trails through and around town.

But it's mountains that really get me thinking. Climbing Mount Lemmon while getting into shape for the 2013 season, I got to thinking of how many mountains I've run through the years. The contrast in terrain after just a few miles of running in Tucson is striking. The trail up Mount Lemmon starts north of Tucson, passing through saguaro and barrel cactus, palo verde trees, all the desert plants people normally associate with Arizona. But it tops out at 9,100 feet, the highest spot in the Santa Catalina range, with evergreens and building storms just like you expect at that elevation. The San Francisco Peaks in Flagstaff and Mammoth Mountain in northern California are higher, but Mount Lemmon gave me heights to strive for in my early days of running.

I can't help but think of Coach Murray when I run in Tucson. The town is surrounded by mountains on all four sides. We met in the Tucson Mountains to the west, close to where I live now and where I've run along trails high on Sentinel Peak and along the Santa Cruz River. On the northern edge of town, I've been all over the Phoneline Trail, Seven Falls, and other routes in Sabino Canyon and along the Rillito Wash that Coach laid out for me. Over Redington Pass in the northeast corner of Tucson is the Rincon Mountains heading south, and then the Santa Ritas in the distance south of town. Everywhere I go in town, I hear Coach Murray's voice.

There's no one I've stayed in closer contact with as an adult. I travel plenty, so a lot of those communications are phone, texts, email, and WhatsApp, but back in Tucson, I always reconnect with Coach Murray in person. I've spent Thanksgiving and Christmas with him more than once. Coach says it feels like I'm his son, and his five grandkids feel like I'm an uncle or a brother. They're all in Tucson, now teens or early 20s, and I truly have seen them grow up.

When it comes to University of Arizona running history, it may sound a little bit like bragging, but I feel like Coach is a link between George Young and me. Before becoming a successful coach at Central Arizona College in Casa Grande, Young graduated from U of A and made it to four Olympics from 1960–72. Coach Murray was a 440-yard runner at U of A, a couple years behind Young. He told me that Young was as mentally tough as any runner he's ever seen and that he trained harder than anybody around him. Young worked for what he got, and that's what I want people to say about me. They can call me a goof-off, or laid back, or fun-loving . . . that's all true, to a point. But I want people to understand that I can be all of that and also get the job done. Coach Murray gave me space to embrace my talent on my terms. That meant finding the right balance between wasting opportunities by not taking running seriously enough and focusing too much on running at the expense of other interests.

Some people have said to me that I should have been more consistent with my training program when I was younger. I should have gotten more out of my talent, they say, or made a commitment to either the track or marathons instead of dabbling in both for so long. I shouldn't have gone to parties, I should have stayed focused on my career by joining a pro team, I should have left Tucson and moved somewhere else. I should have been this or should have done that. What is their point? People sell their house, then when real estate prices skyrocket they wish they could have it back so someone could pay them more. People wish they'd bought Microsoft stock when it first became available. I don't regret my choices. Looking back all the time is the worst thing you can do. We all make mistakes, but we don't get do-overs. If do-overs were that easy, everybody would use them. That's not the way the world works. You make decisions and then you try to make better ones the next time around.

Implied in this criticism is that my coach should have kept me on track. I will always defend Coach Murray when people say I should have trained a different way. He made sure when I was young that Coach Bob Larsen kept an eye on me when I traveled to Mammoth Lakes, but Coach Murray has also always trusted me to live my life as I choose. Through the years, he has given me the freedom and responsibility to set my workout schedule while also keeping up with my health, fitness, and state of mind even if he was 10 time zones away.

When I was inducted into the Pima Community College Hall of Fame in 2013, I wanted to give my coach and town as much credit as I could:

> I transferred to Arizona, where I met my mentor and my father figure to me, Coach Dave Murray. He has done a lot for me, not just as a runner but as a normal human being. He became a father figure to me and helped me out as a person. I've always said that if you have success, that success depends on the people you surround yourself with. As athletes, we do the hard work, but sometimes you go through the tough times. Sometimes you don't want to run or you're in the middle of a race and it's not going the way I wanted. There's so many times that I just wanted to retire from running, but Coach Murray was always there for me as a father figure, as a friend, as anything you could want in a human being. . . .

I also want to thank the Pima [Community College] Hall of

Fame for inducting me. This is an honor and a privilege and I'm so thankful to be a part of it. Whenever I'm traveling around the world, if I'm away for a month or two, I always want to come back to Tucson, because there's no place like home and Tucson is the best place for me.

Most importantly, I think, Coach Murray showed me very early on by example and demeanor the habits and guidelines that helped my performance and my life. Looking back, not only has this ensured I could run successfully for a long time, mostly injury-free and clear-headed, it's meant that I've had a lot more fun and personal investment in my successes and failures along the way. If that's not coaching, I don't know what is.

Coach Murray has never gone to the Olympics with me. I've always told him I'd pay his way to any meet or race, but he's rarely taken me up on it. "That would be like charging my son," he says. And besides, he adds, the coach's work is done before the race. Coach also admits that he gets nervous for me and doesn't want me to take on any of his anxiety.

$$\tilde{\jmath} \; \tilde{\jmath} \; \tilde{\jmath}$$

Below are my habits for living a happy running life, though to be honest, I have never written them down like this before. I know most of these ideas stem from Coach Murray's influence. Time and again over two decades, I've seen the benefits of following these guidelines borne out. See if you agree. I have plenty of friends and competitors who take nutrition, planning, strategizing, data-recording, all of this, much more seriously. For me, though, I want to last a long time on this Earth, and emphasizing simplicity and consistency helps me do that. These guidelines have been tested or affirmed many times. I've done well using this approach throughout my career.

With that, I present to you "Abdi's Habits for Happiness and Success." As far as I'm concerned, you can't have one without the other.

Rock steady. People overestimate the happiness they will feel when they get something they want, whether achieving their goals or buying something important to them. And when things don't go their way, they too easily choose not to look at the steps necessary to feel better again. The reality is, life is constantly in motion; I do my best not to get too high or too low. Disappointment and happiness are fleeting, and you need to overcome both. A *Runner's World* article once said that my "outlook on running embodies Rudyard Kipling's admonition to 'Meet with triumph and disaster, and treat those two imposters just the same.'" Another quote that embodies this thinking is from a medieval Persian poet: "This too shall pass." That's true . . . whether you make the Olympics or DNF because of an injury . . . whether you buy an expensive car or live on a friend's couch.

Practice balance. I am fortunate to still be racing after all these years, but I know I'll keep running long after I stop getting paid to do it. I love to run, and I also like my life off the trails, roads, and tracks. If you are too single-minded about your interests or take yourself too seriously, you'll miss the humor and kindness all around you.

Stick with what works. I don't overthink my race or training strategy; I show up to compete against whoever is there and adjust as the race develops. I don't change coaches every other year. Look at Meb and Coach Larsen, Kip and Coach Li, and me and Coach Murray. We all stayed with our college coaches throughout our entire pro careers, which built trust and confidence. I eat like a normal person. Just because I'm a professional runner doesn't mean I'm eating lettuce all day. In fact, a long time ago, Kip and I decided we would reward our bodies with good food because we push our bodies so hard. I like to have my brain free to explore whatever it feels like and my stomach allowed to consume whatever it craves without overthinking it.

Play the long game. I've found it's a good strategy after each competitive season to make sure I enter the next year fresh. When the season ends, I let it go. It's tempting to focus on what went wrong and figure you can do extra work in the off-season to correct it. But one bad race or one bad season doesn't mean you fire your coach or drastically change what got you to a level of success. We all give and receive help from others in all sorts of ways, and that gets us through difficult times a lot better than looking for someone to blame or abandoning kindness and generosity. Don't seek out quick fixes. Remember where you came from. When you are hurting, give your body a break. You want to be a source of support for others for a long time; don't jeopardize that.

Give yourself 10 minutes. I love running almost every day that I do it. When I can't get out because of injury or other commitments, I feel a little off. Running gives me internal peace and so many mental and physical benefits. And I get paid to do it, so there is that external motivation too. Even with all that positivity attached to the activity of running, I struggle sometimes to get out the door to do it—a lot more than you might think, actually. Once I'm moving, though, my body loosens up (more slowly as I get older, but it does happen) and the cold or the aches or the worries or the list of to-do's or whatever story in my head that had been telling me I didn't want to run will begin to melt away. The first sweat is when everything starts to shift for me. I call it the magic sweat. The first step of the workout is the hardest of thousands to come. Within 10 minutes, the magic sweat takes over, and I'm always glad I was willing to get there. Each subsequent step gets easier . . . until they get harder, of course, but that's another issue. Congratulations to me, and you, for giving ourselves the gift of the first 10 minutes to clear our heads.

CHASING ABDI

5 Rules to Live By

1. Rock steady.
2. Practice balance.
3. Stick with what works.
4. Play the long game.
5. Give yourself 10 minutes.

☞ ☞ ☞

I brushed off my 2012 shortened Olympic performance with a decent 2013. In order to give my knee a chance to heal, I didn't run any marathons, but the races I ran were consistent, and I didn't feel pain. When you train as hard as I do, you have to listen to your body when you need a break. My training put me ahead of where I'd been midway through the previous Olympic cycle, physically and mentally, and I was gearing up for an outstanding 2014.

One race I knew I would not miss that year was the Boston Marathon. I had never run Boston, which for a marathoner left me open to a lot of teasing from my friends. And for an unfortunate reason, the 2014 Boston Marathon was a different kind of experience. It was emotional for everyone, one year after two homemade bombs went off near the finish line, killing three people and injuring hundreds more.

I had originally planned on running Boston in 2013, but I withdrew because of the flu. Friends of mine who were there that year told me what a chaotic scene it was, with people being treated by medical staff at Copley Square and sections of the street near the finish line cordoned off like the crime scene it was. They also talked about feeling fear in an event that is supposed to be free and open to all. Anybody who has ever run or watched a big-city marathon knows the energy all along the public streets of a 26.2-mile course. The hashtag #Boston Strong was the symbolic slogan the resilient Boston community adopted to overcome that fear and hold their event again, and I was honored to be part of it.

It was a historic year, as Meb Kefleghizi set a personal best and became the first American man to win Boston since 1983. Meb ran a fantastic race, taking the lead in the first third of the race and then hanging on by 11 seconds as Wilson Chebet of Kenya closed fast. His countrymen behind him had a good day as well. Ten of the top 20 finishers were Americans, and I was 16th in 2:16:06.

When Meb took off, no one went with him. I always am up for going to the front and trying to drop people, but what he did seemed nuts. There was talk afterward about how we Americans had tried to help Meb

159

by not getting lured into pushing the pace and acting as rabbits for the Kenyan runners wanting to bring him back to the pack. I'd be lying if I said I was racing to help Meb. If I felt like I could have maintained the tempo, I would have worked my way to the front much earlier. Shortly after the halfway mark, I was getting antsy and I think so were other Americans. The Kenyans would put in mini-surges, and I was ready to go. Ryan Hall cautioned me and other Americans to keep a steady pace. If they want to try to reel him in, he said, make them do the work. Sometimes in a marathon, your head isn't entirely there. If people talk, I may listen and I may not. That day, it felt right, and so I did. It's true that those of us in the chase pack ignored the Kenyan mini-surges, and I suppose that did help create a gap for Meb.

At the end of the day, marathoning is still an individual sport, and I came to win. Meb is the one who took the risk of making all of us chase him, and he deserved the rewards, 100 percent. When I realized that Meb had won, it didn't surprise me. I'm never shocked at what Meb can accomplish. The way he did it, though? Man, that was special.

ぎ ぎ ぎ

As the weather warmed up and I returned to Flagstaff, I could always count on seeing new faces on the trails and roads and coffeehouses where runners hang out. In summer 2014, one of those runners was Diane Nukuri. I had met her briefly in 2000, when my University of Arizona teammate Patrick Nduwimana introduced me to Diane and other Burundi Olympians in Sydney. I met her again in 2011 at the historic Falmouth Road Race on Cape Cod, and I would see her occasionally at events, including at the 2012 London Olympics where she carried the Burundi flag for a second time. But we didn't really talk much until she relocated to Flagstaff.

She was in the middle of running four marathons that year and decided Flag was where she wanted to train. The only person she knew very well in town was Janet Cherobon-Bawcom, a Kenyan-born American who placed 12th in the 10,000m in London, so I introduced her to my friends in town. By then, that was a pretty big number of people.

We would all hang out together, walking around downtown Flagstaff, cooking barbecue, whatever. But I definitely wanted to get to know her better. She was beautiful, outgoing, and kind, and she laughed easily. She also seemed to like my odd sense of humor; it just gave her that much more opportunity to tease me. I asked her out a lot, and she said no for a long time—I was definitely the one doing the chasing! But she was always kind when she declined, telling me she was happy being friends. We had many of the same friends in common, so we still saw each other a lot and got to know each other better.

By mid-2015, more than a year after she moved to town, it seemed clear to me we were both interested in developing more than just a friendship, but we hadn't said so to each other or anybody else. That August, I caught Diane (and myself) off guard when I did both of those things at the same time. We were both in Falmouth, which is a special race to both of us. It's where we reacquainted ourselves in 2011, and it's a great setting in a community that really caters to the elite runners who get invited to participate. We even stay with host families when we're there, and when we got together with our hosts that year, I introduced her as my girlfriend. When we returned to Arizona, we announced it to our friends, who wondered what took us so long.

I had a sore hamstring and had to drop out of the race, while Diane won the women's division and my good friend and Tucson training partner Stephen Sambu won the second of his four straight Falmouth titles. At the postrace party, we were having a great time. Lots of people stopped by to congratulate Diane, and she worried that I would be down that I didn't have a good race too. I said, "No way, have fun!" She later told me that she loved the way I didn't let a disappointing race put me in a bad mood, and how I was as excited for her as if I had won. Of course I was happy for her. She deserved to have people recognize her victory . . . and I would have plenty of other races to run.

I never dated much before I met Diane, but she was different. We have lots in common as athletes who are hyper-focused on training. When we compete in the same races, we barely even see each other until the competition is over. But when it is, we explore the cities and eat great food.

More than that, we seem to just understand each other. She motivates me to become more aware of what she wants and to be more responsive to her, as well as other people around me.

When Diane finally decided to go out with me and we started dating, I told her that running was the most important thing to me. She turned to me with a shocked look on her face and shot back, "If that's the case, I'm out."

"No, no, no, that's not what I meant," I replied.

I knew she was joking, but she also was making a serious point. Thank goodness we were able to talk it through. Anybody who has ever trained for the Olympics knows that going after that goal can be terrible for having a balanced life. I think I've handled that tension pretty well, but Diane has been a good example for me too. She wanted me to know that even though we both have been fortunate enough to have this career longer than most, running doesn't last forever. Relationships with family and friends do, and I need to prioritize the important people in my life.

She often helps me be more considerate. I don't like texting, for example; I like to hear people's voices. But sometimes I can wait too long to acknowledge someone is trying to reach me before I get a chance to call. One time I was about to call my chiropractor in Flagstaff, Wes Gregg, to set up an appointment. She said, very kindly, that I probably should text him because he might be working with a client. It was a small thing, but OK, she's right: there's a time to text and a time to call.

I'd like to say Diane has made me more romantic, but I don't know about that. One time, she was doing some modeling for a boutique in downtown Flagstaff. I came by to get her at the end of the photo shoot, and she pointed out a sweater she liked. Later that week, I went back and bought it and asked the owner to keep it there, then told Diane that the owner needed to talk with her. When she went back, the owner explained that the sweater was hers. I don't do those kinds of things often enough—if she asks why we're eating out rather than having a candlelight dinner, I'll say "We'll do that next week." But it's a start.

I like that we don't try to change each other's personalities. Diane says it wouldn't be fun if we just tried to change our partner to be like us. Then they wouldn't be who we fell in love with. Diane, like others I've spent a lot of time with through the years, now that I think about it—Mo Farah, Anthony Famiglietti, and Ryan Shay, just to name a few—is much more outspoken than I am. I will walk away from an argument. She says what she's thinking and stands up for what she believes. I admire that about her, and yet I know that is not comfortable for me. It takes all kinds of people to make the world work, and I see this as yet another way that we learn from each other.

CHASING ABDI

When I first moved to Flagstaff, a guy in my neighborhood used to look at Abdi weird. Turns out they were in the same class at University of Arizona. The guy was super nice. I was there by myself one time and the guy was chatting with me and telling me how smart Abdi is. Abdi walks around and he doesn't present himself as a super smart guy, but this guy said he did a group project with Abdi at U of A. You know how group projects go. You expect to do your part and someone takes the lead. He said Abdi would take everything and make sure it got done right. I said, "What? Abdi's smart!?"

I was kidding. I know how he is. Abdi is really good with numbers. He knows all the politics in Africa, Asia. He reads BBC News every single morning. He knows movies. He collects information. That's Abdi. People don't know that about him. He's very neat and organized in whatever he does. Stuff may be out but it's folded. His car is clean. Languages: Somali, even though he was young when he came. Swahili, he still is fluent because he talks to Kip. He speaks a little Arabic. He's not fluent, but he understands some of it. He's good at languages.

—Diane Nukuri, professional runner and my partner

Even our crazy journeys to reach North America became another opportunity to talk about how fortunate we are to be doing what we love after difficult childhoods. She didn't start running until shortly before the 2000 Olympics, then defected from Burundi after taking a bronze medal in the 10,000m at the 2001 Francophone Games in Ottawa, Canada. Burundi was in the middle of its own civil war that stemmed from the fighting between Hutu and Tutsi tribes in Rwanda, and her father had already died in the conflict. She was granted asylum and stayed with relatives near Toronto, learning English before starting an outstanding collegiate career at Butler County (Kansas) Community College and the University of Iowa.

Diane and I had a strong connection that evolved slowly and has become something very different the more we continue. The best view comes after the hardest climb. While I saw Diane as very much a part of my future, at the same time I was preparing, finally, to return to my roots and experience mountain running on a continent I hadn't seen in more than 20 years.

14

A RETURN
TO ROOTS

"Hey Abdi, you should join me in Ethiopia."
Mo Farah, fresh off his epic double-gold performance on his home London turf, had started going to Africa for training camps and thought I would be interested.

"Nah," I said. "I have what I need in the U.S. I'm busy. My training routes and my friends are there. Have fun."

Some might say if Mo invites you to run with him, don't make him ask twice. But he asked me numerous times in 2013 and 2014, and I kept saying no. I don't make changes when things seem to be working, and I was comfortable with my Tucson-in-winter/Flagstaff-in-summer arrangement.

Besides, Mo knows to respect his elders . . . and I've got him by six years. I've known Mo since he was a teenager. He ran the junior race for the United Kingdom when I was on the U.S. team at the World Cross Country Championships in Portugal in 2000. We had a lot in common and hit it off even then. His family came from Somaliland. When he was a little boy, they escaped Mogadishu around the same time my family did, then spent time as refugees in Djibouti. Only three siblings were able to seek asylum in the UK, so he was separated from his twin brother at age eight and didn't see him for 12 years. We understood each other.

༘ ༘ ༘

I finally decided to join Mo's altitude camp in the mountains of Ethiopia in 2015. I felt like I needed a kick in the butt heading into the 2016 Olympic Trials. From a competitive perspective, I could have made the decision much earlier, but the timing hadn't made sense to me before. Now I was getting older and still training mostly alone. I was in danger of letting the familiar routine lead me into a rut, and I wanted the intensity and consistency of training partners.

Mo's gold medal performances in the 5000- and 10,000-meter races at the 2012 Olympics made him a legend on the track, but he actually made his marathon debut in London in 2014—a week before Meb's Boston victory—so we would now be able to tackle workouts together. Another Somali-born track star, Bashir Abdi of Belgium, was also making his transition to the roads. He had already been in Flagstaff for an altitude camp, so I knew how hard he trained. This group would push me every day, and I would do the same for them.

From a personal perspective, it was bittersweet. Once I made my decision, the thought of seeing Ethiopia, which borders Somalia, got me excited. I had never been back to Africa since we left Kenya when I was 16. Even though I was curious about seeing the continent again, my last memories of Somalia were of being uprooted and confused, not fun times with my friends. I wondered how much of my reluctance to return to my roots was based on not wanting to relive those memories. Mogadishu was still dangerous, but Hargeisa in the north where I still had distant relatives was a safe place. That first year at Mo's camp, though, I only spent time in Ethiopia to train. I talked on the phone with family in Hargeisa, but I decided I would wait until another trip to go back to Somalia. One step at a time for this American.

Once I got to Ethiopia, I wondered why I had even bothered. The hot water would turn off unexpectedly. Wi-Fi was unreliable. My stomach wasn't used to the food. Even the trails we ran on were too rocky for me. I felt like I spent all my attention trying to avoid stepping on boulders. I was being a baby, to be honest. Mo and Bashir let me know it, too. I was taking the conveniences of home for granted. I guess I shouldn't have been surprised that when you get out into the remote areas where we were, you don't have everything available whenever you want it. But this was the first time in a long time that I experienced it firsthand.

𝒮 𝒮 𝒮

My last memory of Africa was getting on a plane in Mombasa to come to the United States with my family. I looked down as the seemingly endless Indian Ocean fell behind us and we flew over the mountains rising above the Rift Valley. This was my first airplane ride, and I felt like a bird. Maybe it sounds strange, but I knew I would miss Mombasa. We had been there more than two years by then; after everything we'd been through, that stability was enough to make me feel comfortable.

We basically hit the lottery—our number came up in a refugee program, and we were headed to Tucson. We could have been assigned to many places in the country, including much colder cities. Instead, we would be living somewhere with warm temperatures not that much different from Somalia and Kenya. As someone who many times has scurried back to Tucson whenever Flagstaff temperatures get below freezing or snow is in the forecast, I can't tell you how grateful I am for our landing where we did.

We had first arrived in Mombasa because my baby sister was born severely premature and the smaller city of Malindi didn't have the medical facilities to give her a decent chance to live. She was transferred to Mombasa, where she stayed on an incubator for several months. While my sister learned to breathe on her own in the hospital, my parents and the five of us learned how to live in a new country.

Being in a refugee camp may not sound like home, but in some ways it very much felt like one. I want to be very clear: my experience was not nearly so desolate as that of someone like Lopez Lomong. For starters, I had my whole family with me. And while the makeshift structures on the giant open lot were crowded, we had a measure of privacy, as well as thousands of Somalis stuck in similar circumstances, who constituted an extended family. It didn't matter whether they were Isaaq or one of dozens of other clans. We were in this together, and we weren't looking for luxury.

We caught a break when we found out my mother had clan relatives in Mombasa. They let us stay in a room of their house, which felt pretty luxurious compared to our camp setup. I remember sticking photos of Muhammad Ali on the covers of my schoolbooks. I considered Ali a hero, and I'll never forget how at my first Olympics in Sydney, he visited with the American team. When I got my photo taken with him, I wanted to tell him about those pictures of him when I was a teenager in my second country, but I was nervous and there were many athletes who still wanted to get a photo with the legendary boxer. He was shaking, his Parkinson's disease well advanced by then, four years past his unforgettable torch lighting at the Atlanta Olympics. Still, he had as commanding of a presence as any person I've ever been around.

Being around Kenyan kids in Mombasa, I got pretty good at speaking Swahili. It's been a point of pride to keep that skill through the years when I meet Kenyan and Tanzanian runners. But I didn't know any English. When we saw cars, we would yell out, "Zoom, zoom," and that was the extent of it. When my parents found out we might get permission to move to the United States, I realized how nervous I was about the need to learn another new language, and in a country where not nearly as many people had my skin color.

My mother has always thanked Allah for the outstanding care she and her baby girl received when we arrived in Malindi and then for the long hospital stay in Mombasa. Near the end of our stay in Mombasa, the two of them took a trip together back to Malindi. Mom and Giannina—the Italian woman who made sure they got safely from the boat to the hospital in Malindi—had stayed in touch a little bit. Now, Mom wanted to introduce our family's angel to a young Giannina. My parents had named my sister the "miracle child" after her, for the help she provided at a time of critical need. Unfortunately, when Mom and my sister, by then 1 1/2 years old and walking, got to Malindi, they were told Giannina was back in Italy. That meant that our newfound friend and her namesake never got to meet again in person. But my family has never forgotten Giannina's kindness.

A RETURN TO ROOTS

We left Kenya on November 24, 1993, and were on planes for close to 24 hours. By the time we arrived in the United States, our new country was celebrating Thanksgiving. We were too tired, confused, and busy trying to get settled in to pay any attention to the holiday. We did find it odd that people were so excited to eat a bird that wasn't a chicken, but we didn't give it much more thought than that. I don't remember if we ate turkey ourselves, but I do remember devouring my first Burger King Whopper a few days later and thinking it was the most delicious thing I'd ever eaten.

We were assigned to low-income housing; I remember a lot of Vietnamese people living around us and only one Somali family nearby in those first few years. I can't say I felt thankful. Our first weeks after leaving Somalia in 1991 certainly didn't feel like just an odd family adventure anymore; it had been hard. But starting over felt even more overwhelming.

My mom tells me that since I was the oldest, I felt my parents' struggles more intensely and so transitions are harder for me. Even though my brothers and sisters were surely sad and sometimes frightened, they were young enough to go with the flow, while I might have internalized my mom and dad's stress. I think she may have a point. I pay attention to the news of the world. I read BBC News online and listen to National Public Radio pretty much every day. I am fully aware of the escalation of the chaos that engulfed Somalia for the next two decades after we left, but I don't dwell on it. Also, I talk to my mom a lot, especially when I'm going through tough times. Everybody should be fortunate enough to get to talk to their mom. But I don't ask much about those years, and I think my parents would rather somehow protect us from those memories. The less we know about the atrocities, the less we have to forget what we don't know.

United Somali Congress rebels entered Mogadishu in December 1990 and toppled Mohamed Siad Barre in January, which is when we left. This led to even more instability all over the country as many groups tried to establish power. In the north, which Siad Barre had devastated with his genocide, SNM rebels declared the independent Republic of Somaliland. Heavy fighting in Mogadishu continued into 1992 and 1993, until U.S.-led United Nations troops arrived. We were a month away from leaving

Kenya when the infamous Black Hawk Down episode occurred in which bodies of American troops were dragged through the streets of the capital. For many years, Mogadishu was regularly considered one of the most dangerous cities on earth.

Do you see why I talk with Meb about getting a second breath? I've continued to do so with Mo, Bashir—who left Mogadishu at age eight and then was a refugee in Djibouti and Ethiopia until his mom was able to bring her husband and kids with her to Belgium—and others. The conversations help me understand what it means to represent my new country in a very tangible way, in a uniform that thankfully is for athletics rather than the military. I wonder why we were able to leave a country that was destroying itself while many others died, or languished in refugee camps in neighboring countries for far longer than I did. We all have our own stories, and to experience them together—even if the details are usually painful and left unstated—is to feel some comfort in familiarity. It makes the miles we run feel not quite so difficult.

My parents were smart and pragmatic. They knew we would be safer overseas than in our home country, and they got their kids to safety. Their reward for their courage was to find it hard to adapt to a new land and language, practicing a religion that some look at skeptically. It can't be easy watching your children grow up as Americans while you struggle to find your footing.

𝒮 𝒮 𝒮

I do want to clarify something: sometimes, because I have an unusual name for the United States, people assume I grew up in the mountains of Kenya. There are many world-class distance runners from the highlands of the Rift Valley. Fans of the sport know about how many great distance runners come from this region whose fault lines slice through multiple countries in east Africa. Starting like a funnel at the Red Sea with Eritrea and Djibouti, the Rift Valley moves south into Ethiopia, down through Kenya, Tanzania, and Mozambique.

I mention this geography because the Rift Valley doesn't even include Somalia. Actually, the Rift Valley essentially cuts off the Horn of Africa—where Somalia sits—from the rest of the continent. When people talk about how the Rift Valley is like an assembly line for incredible runners, they usually mean the Kalenjin ethnic group in western Kenya and the Oromo of Ethiopia, who have led the region's dominance of the sport.

My ethnic group is the Isaaq, which came from Arabia to the east. I was born in Hargeisa, which is in the highlands at 4,377 feet elevation, but moved to the port city of Mogadishu when I was a baby. So I was a sea-level kid and don't remember going to the mountains until I landed in Tucson.

But so many outstanding distance runners either were born in Somaliland, or were descended from people who were. Mo and Bashir are two of them. So is Abdi Bile, a Somali hero for his 1500m world title back in 1987. So is Mo Ahmed, a Canadian now who was born in 1991; and Hassan Mead, now in American, who was born in 1989.

I know the stereotype is that African-born runners have physiological and cultural advantages: we supposedly have greater aerobic capacity and more slow-twitch muscle fibers, and respond better to endurance training because we grew up at altitude or because we had to run to school and cover large areas to herd cattle or whatever situation sounds exotic in western media. I've seen studies that say many of these natural benefits of the body are simply not proven. It does make sense that the lean body types of many Africans, with proportionally long legs and especially thin lower legs, create better "running economy." That's obviously advantageous for distance running. But this has always struck me as making the result fit the facts rather than finding facts that explain a result. For starters, it ignores the fact that people from these countries don't often have the nutritional riches, and material advantages like good shoes and facilities, that Americans and Europeans do.

When it comes to physical attributes, we don't shrug off the successes of large American farm kids who become offensive linemen in the NFL or petite girls who become gymnasts as *only* being the recipients of natural advantages. I said before that we don't all get to the same starting line in life, in sports or education or a supportive family. That's true with our bodies as well as our societies. What we do with those advantages—and how we respond to our disadvantages—makes us who we are.

I'm no expert in race and genetics, and no way do I want to offend friends of any color or country by saying something controversial on the topic. I stay away from that kind of stuff because it's not good for my body or soul. But unlike when I was figuring out how to run efficiently and intelligently back in college, I have plenty of applied experience to give you my take on the subject now. Here it is: we all have gifts given to us and obstacles to overcome—genetic, societal, educational, familial—and luck plays a part in every life. It takes determination and persistence to become the best you can be at an activity. I've seen plenty of successful runners of many different body types from all corners of the world. I know how hard they work to make the most of what God gave them and to overcome the adversities that life has thrown at them. I've also seen runners try to play God with their bodies and circumvent the fair process of determining winners and losers by doping. Some get away with it; others get caught or injured. I prefer to focus on having fun, playing fair, and taking the long view of success—then enjoy my opportunity to meet people from all walks of life along the way.

𝒳 𝒳 𝒳

In Ethiopia in 2015, I slowly began to find my footing. I laughed a lot and had regular training partners. I was 38 years old and feeling like I was in my 20s. Young runners were everywhere, waking up early to get on the roads with Mo, Bashir, and me, to breathe the same oxygen. I saw hundreds of Ethiopians running through town on any given day who saw running as a means to economic success. Desperation can create a hunger to succeed. Perhaps that's what drove me at first, too, and still does. When I got a chance to run at Pima, I found a place where I *belonged*. I am grateful to still make a living doing what I love, but I guarantee you I wouldn't have lasted 20 years at this if I was just doing it for the money.

CHASING ABDI

Hobbies/interests: I like hanging out with friends. I like photography. I'm not that good yet, but I like taking pictures of landscapes. I don't get to do that too often because when I'm training strong I am always tired and recovering, which limits my walking around.

Favorite movies: Denzel Washington movies—anything with Denzel I love!

Favorite music. U2. I like Bono.

Favorite breakfast: Boiled eggs. Bread with peanut butter and honey.

Favorite meal: I like beef or goat meat stew with rice.

First running memory: I remember when I was young I wasn't the fastest guy, but I was the one who could run the longest. I wasn't a sprinter, but I could keep going.

Running heroes: I look up to Billy Mills—I look at him like he is my running idol. I have a great respect for the sport and people who came before us, like Bob Kennedy, Todd Williams, and Mark Davis. They are all my heroes.

Childhood dreams: Running wasn't one of my dreams. I wanted to be an engineer.

Favorite places to travel: My favorite place to travel in the U.S. is New York City. You can't go wrong with New York City—the greatest city in the world. I also love Arizona.

—From interview with Gary Cohen, November 2014
(garycohenrunning.com)

In Michael Crawley's book *Out of Thin Air: Running Wisdom and Magic from Above the Clouds in Ethiopia*, he writes about the passion for running throughout the country, especially in group workouts. "To be changed you have to run with others," he says. When you take your turn at the front of a training run, you are "bearing someone else's burden," and to follow someone's feet is to feed off their energy.

The inconveniences I originally grumbled about became part of the joy I felt thanks to being away from the rest of the world. I remembered not being all that interested in joining the Mammoth Lakes bunch because it was so remote, then realizing I enjoyed the camaraderie of friends when we were removed from the rest of the world. I like Wi-Fi and fast food, but connections with people are important, maybe even more so in the isolation of the mountains when training and talking take up most of your time.

Ethiopian runners seek out uneven ground, whether to slow the pace or just to have fun. Akaki is just south of Addis Ababa and at more than 6,000 feet elevation. It is a common area for us to go on long runs. One day I was taking my turn in the lead and hammering it, about 19 miles in. I hit a rock and went down hard. Bashir said he thought I had hit my head and was sure I was done, at least for the day. Instead, I was determined to finish strong. They were ready to carry me away and I was barking at them to get back in line.

I needed a change in mindset, and the months I spent working out with those guys gave me peace of mind, confidence, and a strong training base as I returned to the United States for the 2016 Olympic Trials. It seemed that everything was coming together for me to make my fifth Olympic team and have a chance to complete the marathon this time around.

15

HEARTBREAK AND
A NEW YORK REDEMPTION

In mid-January 2016, I agreed to pace a couple of friends who were try-ing to get a qualifying time at the Rock 'n' Roll Arizona Half Marathon. They were looking for a last chance that would allow them to compete at the Olympic Marathon Trials coming up in a month. It was a training run for me and I was looking forward to it, but I tweaked my left calf before-hand and had to back out.

Coach Murray and I thought I could work through it. It was a nag-ging injury, but there was no reason to believe it wouldn't fully heal if given enough rest. My timing was simply awful. This was when I should be doing my final high-intensity work before tapering off for the Trials. We backed off for a while . . . not ideal, but if rest got me to the starting line in Los Angeles, I figured I would be fine and my competitive juices would carry me to the finish. One day led to another, and after 10 days of virtually no work, it was clear I would not be fine. Coach always said that you don't start a marathon if you're only feeling 50 percent healthy. Spiritually it's not showing proper respect for the distance, and physically it's putting your body in jeopardy for a bigger injury.

I know how "in the moment" the U.S. selection system is. You get the job done on the day of the Trials or you stay home from the Olympics—doesn't matter if you're injured or have a stomach bug. I remember Bob

Kennedy bruised his spine in a traffic accident before the 2000 Trials. Even though he was one of the favorites, he had to scratch. I'd been on both sides of the equation that this one-shot approach can create—a surprise top-three finisher or a DNF. But always—always—since 2000, I'd found a way to make the U.S. Olympic team.

Of course, this was devastating news for me. Coming back from Ethiopia, all in as a road racer, I truly believed I would be on the podium. I had high hopes of being the first American distance runner to qualify for five Olympic teams. To be honest, I saw that as part of my legacy in the sport. I didn't know Frank Shorter from Bill Rodgers when I first started running in college, but now the history of American distance running was important to me. Plus . . . Rio. Who doesn't want to go to Rio? I had grown accustomed to being part of the Olympic experience every four years my whole adult life. If there was a way to still make it happen, I wanted to do it.

I could have taken a cortisone shot to mask the pain and kept training. Athletes have done that for years, and some had managed to suit up for big games and races by doing so. It might have allowed me to have a chance at this experience that was so important to me. But I knew that was not the answer. As much as I wanted to make the Olympics, I understood there are bigger things than running in a big race. I pay attention to what my body is telling me. Even if I had taken a painkiller for several weeks and kept my fitness up and managed more than 30,000 strides over 26.2 miles on a sketchy calf muscle to be a top-three finisher, I could have done lasting damage that I wouldn't know about for years. I will retire at some point, and I have no desire to be limping around more than I already do because I made a hasty decision when I was 38. I walk slow enough as it is.

Twelve days before the Trials, I announced that I was scratching.

Everyone around me supported me fully. My family and friends, my coach, my agent, my sponsor. It was unfortunate, and yet I did really the only responsible thing I could. Nothing is more important than staying healthy for the long haul, not even the Olympics.

The next question, beyond giving myself time to heal, was what would the rest of 2016 look like. Doctors said I could be fully recovered in a few more weeks. I considered running a spring marathon, including possibly Boston. With many top runners focused on the Olympic Marathon or Track and Field Trials, that could have even been a fairly lucrative decision. Another consideration was returning to the 10,000m and try to qualify on the track as I had done in 2008. My last track race was five years earlier, but I knew I could get used to the spikes again, the jostling for position and reading the turns. All that had been logged into my muscle memory long ago. A few 3000- or 5000-meter races to get the feel and the confidence of it again was all it would take, I thought. "Everything good comes to an end but this isn't the end," I told SI.com on February 1 when I withdrew. "I just have to focus on the next chapter of my career and gear up for the next marathon and then the 10K."

Ultimately, I decided not to run Boston. My calf muscle didn't fully heal in time, and my training cycle would have been too condensed. I also decided it wasn't a good plan to try and qualify in the 10,000m. I told myself it would be a fun challenge to return to the track, but it felt desperate. Plus, the American field was as strong as it had been in decades. I was a marathoner now. My home was on the roads. When early July rolled around, Galen Rupp cruised to 10,000m victory at the Trials in Eugene with a 27:55.04, followed by Shadrack Kipchirchir (28:01.52) and Leonard Korir (28:16.97). My PR in the 10,000 was 27:16.99, but that was eight years ago. My last 10,000m on the track was five years ago: 28:57.79. Could I have pushed out one of those three? I'll never know, but I'll never regret choosing not to try on that one.

$$\mathcal{F} \; \mathcal{F} \; \mathcal{F}$$

Marathoning is a strange profession. I had considered myself a full-time marathoner ever since London, and yet in the past four years I had only run one of them: Boston in 2014. To love doing something so much but then actually experience it so rarely creates a strange longing in your brain. I did realize during this period how fun it is to run half marathons on the road. We just push, push, push, for a full hour. The additional 13.1 miles of the marathon totally changes the dynamic of a race. Sometimes that can be a welcome challenge, and other times it can just hurt. As with many things in life, when it goes well, you love it and you can't imagine doing anything different. When it's not going well, you wonder why you willingly chose to put yourself in this dilemma. Thankfully, when it's over, my memory is short, so I prepare for the next one with enthusiasm.

While the world's running community looked to Rio, I set my sights on New York . . . again. I've raced more there than in any other city, and more often than not, I've done well. The memory of Central Park at the 2007 Olympic Trials still lingers, though. That will never go away.

I planned to make the New York City Marathon in November my very own Olympics. To prepare, I ran a race a month, starting with the U.S. Half Marathon Championships in Columbus, Ohio, in late April (seventh place, 1:03:49) and ending at the South Shields Great North Run in the United Kingdom in early September (sixth place, a 1:02:46 half marathon). In between, I had top-10 finishes in four famed 10Ks around the United States—Boulder, Boston, Atlanta Peachtree, and Cape Elizabeth, Maine.

I knew I was fit and prepared for NYC 2016, but even more than that, I had peace of mind about where I was at in my career. My disappointment in not keeping my Olympic streak alive had given way to a better understanding of my body. I always tell people age is just a number to me, and that's true. But after training so hard for the Trials, I realized rest is just as important as training. I could no longer do three hard runs a week like I did when I was younger. Maybe I only do one or two. I still liked to set the pace, but I also knew better how to run the race that is best for me.

That became clear midway through the race when Ghirmay Ghebreslassie of Eritrea, Lucas Rotich of Kenya, and Lelisa Desisa of Ethiopia put a move on the rest of the field. I knew if I covered it, I would pay the price later. I'd be crawling to the finish line, if I even made it that far. So I stayed with the chase pack, and with a few miles to go, my focus was on holding off Hiroyuki Yamamoto of Japan, Shadrack Biwott of the United States, and Moses Kipsiro of Uganda, who were all near me. But then I passed Desisa at about 36km, and my eyes got big. I wasn't thinking about fourth anymore. I made a little surge; no one came along. I made another one; still alone. I decided to sustain a longer surge for maybe a half mile or so, and when I did, the gap increased.

CHASING ABDI

Excerpt from "Abdi Abdirahman Still Wins the Party," an article by Sarah Barker in *Deadspin*, September 29, 2016.

Abdi Abdirahman said he is "way more relaxed" at 39 than he was when he was younger, causing me to experience a mutifying, brow-furrowing dissonance.

Even when he was younger, Abdirahman was the sharpest dressed, chillest BMW-driving ladies' man to ever take a day off from running because he didn't feel like it. Among professional distance runners—certainly the lamest partiers in the sports world—the four-time Olympian has always been the standard-bearer for bon vivant. So, *way* more relaxed than that? That's saying something.

Take that image of the nearly pulseless 5'11", 130-pound figure draped over a Barcalounger, and hold it right up next to the one of the same knife-kneed guy sweating, gritting, working the pins over 13.1 miles in 62 minutes and 46 seconds, which he ran just a few weeks ago. Life of the party—4:48 spleen-busting minutes per mile for 13 miles. Eh, not feeling it today—hammering for sixth place in the UK's Great North Run against fellows who take this sort of thing pretty seriously. See the disconnect? A 62-minute half-marathon is not achieved by training when you feel like it.

"Well exactly. I'm not taking it easy. I'm still training hard, maybe harder now," Abdirahman explained. "When I was younger I was chasing my dreams, trying to accomplish things, make teams. Now I'm running for fun, to see how fast I can run, for how long. You just gotta enjoy what you do in life. I enjoyed it before, but I'm enjoying even more now. There's not a lot of pressure to perform."

With two miles to go, I knew I was in good position to take my first-ever podium at New York City. I stayed relaxed and remembered nothing is ever guaranteed in a marathon. I've seen people blow up in the 25th mile. The incredible crowd noise lifted me down the stretch as I finished third in 2:11:23, 26 seconds ahead of Yamamoto. I talked about my long career in an interview after the race:

> For me, I don't think like I'm the oldest. I'm 39 years old. Age is just a number to me, but at the same time, I believe you can do anything you put your mind to. I enjoyed it. It was a great race. I don't look at my age as a disadvantage or advantage. Actually, I kind of look at it as an advantage because I knew the course and I've run it and I've been around a long time. I was telling these guys I was in the Olympics in 2000, and they were looking at me like, 'Really?' And I said, 'Yes.'

Ghebreslassie rolled to the victory. He was only five years old when I ran in my first Olympics. I was asked for any advice I had for him:

> For a long career, don't try to make as much money as you can for one year. That's short and clear because like you can run three marathons and make a lot of money in one year, but your career will be over within three years. If you want to have a long career, longevity, enjoy life, do two or one marathon a year and just enjoy the moment and just make sure you're doing the right training. Stay with the same coach. Have the same routine.

I had just run the third-fastest marathon of my career. I became the oldest male runner in New York City Marathon history to reach the podium and was the first American man to finish in the top three there since Meb won the race in 2009. In sports, you often hear the phrase, "Run your own race," but I don't know if you really start to understand what that means until you get a little older, have had some ups and downs, and know what you want your race to be.

By the end of the 2016 season, I didn't have an Olympic memory, but I was understanding the value of experience—in racing as well as in training. In the past 12 months, I'd come to realize I liked the consistency and camaraderie of regular training partners whom I could help as much as they could help me. I was ready to return to Ethiopia again, and maybe this time, I might add Somalia to my itinerary.

Missed Olympic Ring
Rio de Janeiro

In the days before the Rio Olympics, I was in Flagstaff, training and wondering if it might be miserable watching the track events on TV. It turned out it wasn't bad at all. The Opening Ceremonies were amazing. Turns out the only way Coach Murray can keep me away from them is for me not to qualify. I hung out with my friends and watched other friends, teammates, competitors, training partners, and even my girlfriend get their Olympic moments. It was like I was there! Bernard Lagat qualified for his fifth Olympics—his third as an American and his first without me also there with him. Hassan Mead, a Somali-born naturalized citizen, also qualified in the 5000m with Bernard. Mo Farah repeated his 2012 double-gold in the 5000 and 10,000m, while American Galen Rupp took away a bronze medal in the marathon.

Most importantly, I got to watch Diane Nukuri in her third Olympics for Burundi. Since we go our own ways at big races, it didn't seem all that strange to not be experiencing the Olympics with her. But I enjoyed watching her from afar. She placed 13th in the 10,000m, and I was cheering her the whole way. She left Rio before the Closing Ceremonies so that she could try to defend her title at the Falmouth race. I joined her there. She was third; I was sixth. No one was surprised this time to hear we were dating.

Part VI
Tokyo 2020-21

A LESSON IN UNITY

"Abdi blends in as an American. He respects America;
he's loyal and patriotic. But when we talk about Africa,
his love of Africa also comes through. It's real. He's like me.
I'm an American. I pay taxes and I'm grateful to be here,
but I'm also an African. So is Abdi. We have different
personalities in Africa, just as America does."

—Kip Lagat, my friend and training partner

16

A MASTER
ON TEAM MUDANE

You know why I was excited to return to Ethiopia in early 2017? Two words: camel's milk.

My second trip back to Africa was definitely different than my first time back, two years before—lots to look forward to with not nearly as much anxiety, other than adding a short stay in Somalia this time. This time, I knew the area around Addis Ababa—the 7,500-foot elevation of the Sululta Plain north of the city, the punishing tempo runs in the Akaki woreda to the south, the midafternoon trips to the market for perfect, freshly ground coffee.

And, oh, the camel's milk. Camels are currency in Arab countries and Somalia. They are given away to the bride's family at weddings. When there's a big feast or event, slaughtering a camel is the traditional way to celebrate. Camels aren't so common in Ethiopia, but the Afar are a Muslim clan who raise them, and we found a family that sold camel's milk at the market in Addis.

Camel's milk is the best. It's so creamy, delicious, good for your bones. Like the animal it comes from, the milk is extremely pragmatic. It doesn't have to be pasteurized like cow's milk because it has so much bacteria in it. It can last for weeks without spoiling, and if it gets a little sour, you just shake it up. When I'm in Ethiopia on what has become almost an annual altitude training-camp visit, I drink a glass of camel's milk each night for recovery. I sleep like a baby.

The value of training partners was much clearer to me the second time around, too—not just Mo and Bashir but also the talented pros we invited to join us. Most are originally from Somalia, like Mohamed Ali of the Netherlands, Mustefa Mohamed of Sweden, and Ahmed Osman of the United States, but we get other young runners from Somalia and Ethiopia too.

There's never any shortage of runners in Ethiopia. Thousands of hopefuls embrace the sport. They both respect it as a sacred thing and also want to make a career out of it. They'll hop on buses at 3 a.m. to join a training group. They challenge themselves against runners who are far better than they are so they can see how good they can be when pushed to the test on a workout. After workouts, they listen intently to Bashir and me tell war stories in English or our mediocre Somali (Mo's is a little better), then laugh at our language mistakes. They call me the old man, but they know I've got experience that I'm willing to share—and that I can still keep up with them. I still get the last word most of the time!

It's really not that much different than being on a college sports team. I'm with people whose experiences and interests match mine, at least somewhat. All of us yearn to experience a feeling of belonging, in a place where we can be ourselves. Training camp in Ethiopia is an island of comfort and safety—and if a byproduct of that is a world-class level of fitness, I'll take that too.

In the book *Out of Thin Air*, the Scotsman Michael Crowley captures this dynamic very well. He says that in Europe, athletic potential is seen as individual, self-contained. But in Ethiopia, "energy is seen as trans-bodily. It can flow between people, it can be shared and it can even, on occasion, be stolen."

ℱ ℱ ℱ

With the change in U.S. administrations from President Barack Obama to Donald Trump in early 2017 came an executive order that blocked entry of people from seven nations that were predominantly Muslim, including Somalia, regardless of whether they had valid visas. It affected millions of people, and even though I'm an American citizen, I personally knew people who were worried about the effects of it. Mo, a British citizen who was living in Eugene, Oregon, but of course traveling all over the world, commented on social media that "I will have to tell my children that Daddy may not be able to come home."

Mo is more vocal in expressing his views than I am, but I understood where he was coming from. He had been living in the United States for six years. For him and many others, the order created confusion and chaos. This country that had been so good to me was basically saying that anybody who came from Somalia was suspicious, including Mo, who was a permanent resident of the United States at the time.

A lot of great things happen in this country because of immigrants, and unless you're Native American, you're not full-blooded American. Most of us came from immigrants who were running from or running to something. Or put another way, they came here chasing something or being chased by something. Why assume everyone is trying to start trouble when the vast majority just want to make a better life for themselves and their families? I'm not saying we should have entirely open borders. I don't pretend to know the answers on how to structure the policy. I'm just saying it is a terrible starting point to the discussion when people demonize others they think aren't like them.

Various versions of this ban were attempted during Trump's four years in office, followed by lawsuits to try and stop them from being enforced. The order didn't prevent Mo and me from returning to Ethiopia that spring, but I couldn't help but think that while I was personally and professionally content with my life, a lot of bad energy was brewing all around the country. The world felt like it was shifting quickly and becoming more unstable.

I remembered how my parents talked about how nice Somalia was in the years since it gained its independence in 1960 . . . before it tore itself apart. The government took care of its citizens. The middle class was strong. The president unified the Somali language by having it transcribed for the first time. The benefits of clan life—people looking out for each other, tight-knit communities—gave way to its dangers—finding others who didn't look or believe like you and turning them into enemies. It changed millions of people's lives forever. For a long time, I felt like the African story, whether Burundi, Sudan, Rwanda, wherever, was always some version of the Somalia story: those with power wanted more of it, and anyone who stood up to the bully risked losing everything. The bully may eventually be defeated, as Siad Barre was, but everyone pays a price. And when two groups fight, there is always collateral damage. They will kill people who aren't in their group, whether or not you have a weapon.

As I prepared to return to Africa, I realized these human tendencies, to belong but also to blame, were not isolated to one part of the globe. I resolved again to share positive energy with anybody I came into contact with. Even if I disagree with you about politics, religion, or values, we still are in this life together and can find common ground. I may not change the world in some dramatic way, but I can sure make it a better place for myself and those around me.

𝒵 𝒵 𝒵

In Ethiopia, I felt so much positive energy flowing between my friends and training partners, and after the camp was over I carried that energy in my heart when I made my first trip back to Somalia in 26 years. I had forgotten the details of my life in Mogadishu before the wheels came off, and after all that time it still remained a city in turmoil. On October 14, 2017, just months after I was in the country, almost 600 people died there in terrorist truck bombings. But my visit was to Hargeisa, in Somaliland. I found myself relaxed and at peace in that city.

My mother had taken her five grandchildren and her daughter-in-law there for nearly a year, and I got to see them for a couple of weeks. Mom wanted the young ones to know her homeland, which I guess is also theirs and mine, depending on how you want to look at it. I can't say Somalia necessarily felt like my country, but I knew it was part of me. It was fun to see my mother happy as she introduced me to her friends and relatives. Perhaps my nieces and nephews will choose to go back more often. Maybe they'll take more opportunity to retain the Somali language as I have chosen to do with Swahili, keeping up with Kip Lagat and other Kenyan runners. They have many years to write their story.

Back in the United States, I felt the positive energy in my racing that year too. Even though I entered the master's category when I (according to my official documents) turned 40 on January 1, 2017, I had no intention of being considered anything less than an elite runner. After returning from Ethiopia, I went to Boston and placed sixth and won my first race ever in the master's division.

CHASING ABDI

🐦 David Monti
@d9monti

> After he got 3rd at #tcsnycmarathon last yr, @Abdi_runs pointed at me & said, "Cactus is back!" He'll be back on 11/5.

@JaneMonti1

7:17 AM · Sep 2, 2017

—Tweet from David Monti, New York City Marathon elite coordinator, September 2, 2017

In the fall, I returned to New York City, got tripped as I pulled into a water stop in the third mile, and still placed seventh in 2:12:48, breaking Meb's master's record at the event and winning money in the open and master's categories, as well as for being the first American. With that additional check, maybe I could get used to this master's label after all!

That was yet another memorable day in the Big Apple. Meb had announced it would be his final race as a professional, and he soaked up the congratulations over the last few miles as he placed 11th in 2:15:29. It was a "Mebathon" to remember. We had so many great battles through the years, and I love that guy, just like everyone else does. But to be honest, even on his celebration day I really wanted to beat him. He's the sweetest person in the world. We've roomed and eaten prerace dinners together all over the world. Still, I always say never let him smile at you. He's just softening you up before he tries to bury you. Of course, my friend Mike Smith from Flagstaff, who is now the national championship–winning director of track and field and cross country at Northern Arizona University, says about me that people think I'm laid back when in fact "Abdi's a total killer and he'll cut your head off."

After I fell, my hip and ankle were bruised, but I knew I could press on. I saw Meb up with the lead group and I thought to myself, I want to keep him company as much as I can on his final day at the office. We ran together for a little while . . . but you didn't think I'd let Meb beat me on his big day, did you?

I also felt the positive energy as Diane and I continued to build our relationship. In 2017, she finished ninth at both Boston and New York with 63 seconds separating her two times. My times in both were just three seconds apart. But the real balance we experienced was figuring out how to *be* with each other. We didn't always agree on everything, but most of the time we did. Overall, we found ways to support each other.

$$ \mathcal{Z} \ \mathcal{Z} \ \mathcal{Z} $$

I started 2018 by finishing fifth in the Doha Half Marathon in Qatar before heading back to Ethiopia. Only this time around, Mo had given us a more official title. Two months earlier, Queen Elizabeth had knighted him. That's right: the teenager I met 18 years earlier, this guy who I've had many laughs with that I won't ever tell you about, was now an actual knight. That's what winning four gold medals will do for you.

He showed up with Team Mudane gear for all of us. "Mudane" means "Sir" in Somali, and the name gave us even more of an identity. It solidified the commitment of Bashir, Mo, and me to remember our Somali heritage, which has not always been easy for me. As I discussed with Meb so many years earlier, I felt like my second breath meant something important. We wanted our altitude-training camps to attract young Somali runners who otherwise might not have a chance to make a name for themselves. I was honored to be the senior citizen in this group and to get to work again. As Bashir said, "Abdi could be my dad, but at the same time he's a tough guy. He's still so strong in training. Running means a lot to him. The day he doesn't run, he's a totally different Abdi. When he doesn't run, he says, 'Ah, I don't deserve my food today.' When he runs, he eats good food and tells jokes."

CHASING ABDI

From an interview with Chris Chavez on his Citius Mag podcast in November 2017, just prior to the New York City Marathon.

Chris: We're doing this fun thing on Twitter and all of a sudden people started doing it all across the country. People were running in blue jeans in a mile trying to figure out how fast they could run a mile. We put out a challenge for $1,200 for the first person who could run four in the mile in jeans that were 100% denim. The fastest we saw was a kid from BYU who ran 4:16 at altitude. What are your thoughts? Someday, would it be possible for someone to run four minutes for the mile in a pair of blue jeans?

Me: I think it's definitely possible, but it depends. You have to be specific. What cut of jeans?

Chris: We gave them two inches above the ankle. That's the most you could roll up your jeans.

Me: What is the cut? Skinny cut? Loose fit?

Chris: Two guys ran 4:16 and it was a bigger cut at the bottom. A little baggier.

Me: I think it's doable. You put the right person and the right cut, I think it's doable.

Chris: What's the fastest you think you could do in blue jeans, because you haven't broken four straight?

Me: I think I could do under 4:20.

Chris: Breaking Two. You were able to watch it on a livestream. You've raced Eliud [Kipchoge] before. How much of a freak is he?

Me: He's an amazing athlete. That day, my respect went through the roof. I need to come up with a nickname for him. That was amazing, something out of this world. That motivates me to keep going. I know him well, and the way he's running, what he's doing and capable of doing, why would I put limits on myself?

Chris: He seems like the most peaceful guy. Everything he says could be a quote on a T-shirt or a tattoo. It seems like the guy operates at peace.

Me: Sometimes it sounds like it's not even real what he says. Even if you have a normal conversation with him, the way he answers you, it's inspiring and it moves you. You think, he just said that to me?

Chris: Bernard Lagat loves his golf. What do you love?

Me: (laughing) I love hanging out with my friends, to be honest. That's most important to me. I like barbecuing. I like cooking. I like making beef stews, lamb stews, goat stews. I tried to become a golfer like Bernard, but I got bored.

Chris: The Steelers are killing it. You're a big fan.

Me: They're 6-2, and their bye week is next week so they're staying home to watch the New York City Marathon that I'm going to win. That's why they get the bye week.

Chris: Do you think you could beat [Steelers wide receiver] JuJu Smith-Schuster down the field if you both started in the endzone, all the way down to the other end of the field?

Me: He would smoke me. That 28-year-old guy. I could be his daddy. I definitely would race him in the 800 meters though. That would be a good race.

Chris: If enough people tweet this out, we could get the Steelers to set this up. A big thing we did, again on Twitter, was LeBron vs. Malcolm Gladwell, he's 54 years old, famous writer, but he's run a 4:57 for the mile. The big debate was what could LeBron James run in the mile? You said you and JuJu would be competitive at 800 meters. What do you think LeBron would run for the mile?

Me: I don't think LeBron could run 5:30.

Chris: Really? Dude, I could run 5:30.

Me: Chris, look at how big you are and look how big LeBron is.

Chris: LeBron is one of the most talented athletes in the world. And there's some high school kids who can run sub-5. Mediocre high school kids can run sub-5.

Me: Running is different, Chris. That's what you're missing. LeBron is one of the most talented athletes in the world. We know that. Jumping, dunking, running 50 meters, 10 meters. Look how big the basketball court is. LeBron can take four or five steps. But four laps around the track. If he breaks 5:30, I'd be so surprised. I'll give LeBron 5:50. I have seen it. I have friends who played basketball and have almost the same build as LeBron. There's no way they run 5:30.

Chris: Oh man, there's guys at UNC [University of North Carolina], they do it every year, they run the mile just to see how fast they can run and their times are something like low 5s.

Me: It must not be a power forward or a center. It must be shooting guards or point guards.

Chris: I'm looking it up right now. Luke May won last year in 5:06. He's a big guy. I think he's a forward.

Me: Is he 240?

Chris: Luke May is 6' 8", 240.

Me: And he ran 5:06?

Chris: Yeah.

Me: Holy cow. OK.

Chris: I think sub-5 is possible.

Me: We don't know exactly. But for me, if I see somebody's body, I can always tell how fast they are capable of going if they train for it. But just looking at LeBron and the way he walks and his build? I don't know. [My best outdoor mile is 4:06.93 at the Drake Relays in 2002.]

$\mathcal{F}\ \mathcal{F}\ \mathcal{F}$

After three months in Ethiopia, I returned to sea level in time for the 2018 Boston Marathon and I was fit and lean, man. I was planning on a top-five finish. Instead, I was running in the worst weather since the 2001 World Cross Country Championships. I don't like chilly weather, as my Flagstaff friends will tell you when I leave town suddenly to avoid a cold snap. But I'm not afraid of it either; I can handle wind, rain, and cold. On Patriots' Day that year, though, we got all three, and I wasn't prepared for that. Even at high elevation in Addis Ababa, nighttime temperatures rarely got below 50 degrees Fahrenheit. I don't think I had experienced freezing temperatures in a full year. If there was ever a day for DNFs, this was it: constant rain in near-freezing conditions, with 25 mph headwinds and gusts into the 30s.

Here's how I described it to Sarah Barker of *Deadspin*:

"It was brutal. I wore a T-shirt under my singlet, and arm warmers. I don't honestly know why I did that because everything was soaking wet right away, and stayed wet. I was shivering, freezing cold. I was running slow but I was extremely tired, my quads were tired, my joints were cold, I wasn't moving. I tried but I just couldn't move. At every single water stop I thought about dropping out."

"Why didn't you?" she asked.

"I know how much work I put into [preparation for] this race. And I was not doing as bad as anyone else . . . I don't know why. I just don't like to DNF. I wasn't having a great day, but for me, I just don't like to DNF unless it's absolutely necessary. Giving up is not a good thing. Thirty kilometers to 35, that was brutal. But when I got to 38K, I thought about how far I'd already come and I thought, 4K to go—why quit now? I wanted to finish; that was my goal."

Back when I was training with Meb and his coach, Bob Larsen, at Mammoth Lakes, Coach Larsen would say, "Abdi might forget his shoes or his shorts, but if you get him to the starting line he's got a chance to do something special." If anything, I would have been better to forget extra clothes that day, but my soaked shoes, shorts, and self completed the 42 kilometers.

I finished in 2:28:18, which actually was good enough for 15th place and another master's victory on that crazy day. I've never focused on time as much as place, but for some reason, when I crossed the finish line and glanced at the clock, 2:55 flashed in front of me. Perspective is everything. After misreading that, 2:28 felt just fine. Anyway, I'd rather have a slow recorded time than a DNF. I knew I did my best on a day when I could have easily quit.

$$\mathscr{F} \; \mathscr{F} \; \mathscr{F}$$

I say without any hesitation that I know I would have been on the podium in 2016. I don't know who would have stayed at home, but I was convinced that had I been able to show my best at the Trials, I would have qualified for Rio. If I had made my fifth Olympics in 2016, I don't know if I would have continued to compete and try again four years later. Being the first American distance runner to qualify for five Olympic Games was a goal of mine, and if I'd satisfied that itch in 2016, would I have kept scratching? But this is another example of why it's better to live the life you're given than nurse your regrets, because I was grateful for all that happened in my career after 2016. The 2020 Trials were now in my sights, and my training was as strong as ever. I was also more selective in my races, in order to give myself time to recover.

I had plenty of motivation to push for another Olympics. I would officially be 43 when the Trials came around, and I really believed I might break some hearts. I've always said everybody is entitled to their own opinion and I'm entitled to show I'm still in the hunt. I have more fun now than ever—and that's saying something.

When Hannah Borenstein of *Podium Runner* asked me weeks before the 2020 Trials what I would do if I made the Olympic team, I was in Ethiopia. For some reason, I thought of how resilient camels are. They're called in Swahili "Safina Sahara" . . . the "ship of the desert." Having flat feet rather than hooves makes them more useful than horses in sand, rocks, any tough terrain. They can handle extremes in weather over long distances without water—and even be fast for short stretches when they need to be. And oh, that milk. I was ready for some right then.

If I win, I said, "I just want to have a big party at my house. I want to have all my friends over. And I want to slaughter a camel."

Was I kidding? I have no idea. I just know I never got the chance to have my big feast.

17

OLD MAN KICKING IT
IN ATLANTA

We were just starting our third eight-mile lap onto Peachtree Street, less than 10 miles from the finish, when Galen Rupp took charge of the U.S. Olympic Marathon Trials. He had taken the lead on a chilly, windy Leap Day in 2020 and looked like a puppy, boundless energy, just waiting for someone to come along with him to play.

Then we made one of the dozens of tight turns on the downtown Atlanta course and he practically came to a standstill. "Let's go, guys. Do your part in cutting this wind with me and I'll carry you to the finish," he seemed to be saying.

What I think he actually said was much more succinct but no less clear: "C'mon."

I was more than happy to shoulder my share of the load. I had made a couple of mini-surges earlier in the race, and I knew I needed to put a gap between me and some of the young guns in the lead pack, like Leonard Korir and Augustus Maiyo, if I was going to have a chance at a top-three finish. What better way to do that than by joining Galen, the defending Trials champion, three-time Olympian, and bronze medalist at the 2016 Rio Games.

I quickly shuffled to the front with him. If Galen wanted the field to chase him, I've always been happy to play that game.

That decision came with a risk, though. There was plenty of time to blow up if I had taken off too soon, and Rupp had just laid out back-to-back 4:51 and 4:57 miles. I knew I couldn't expect to maintain that pace for another 50 minutes. Maiyo, Korir, and Matt McDonald soon joined us. Within another half mile, it appeared to be a five-man race. A mile after that, by the 18-mile mark, Korir had fallen back and there were four of us. Might this be a replay of the final third of the 2012 Olympic Trials, when Meb, Ryan Hall, and I managed to hold off Dathan Ritzenhein for the three Olympic spots?

𝒳 𝒳 𝒳

Much more so than at the start of the century, the U.S. Marathon Trials are a publicized and highly anticipated event. Since 2012, the men and women run the same course on the same day for maximum media coverage. It becomes a must-see event on the running calendar every four years. Commentators are everywhere—podcasts, websites, magazines, television. . . everyone who cares about the sport has a take. They make their lists and decide who is most likely to make the team. If I thought these people had forgotten about me at the 2012 Trials, I was truly invisible in 2020. The field was the largest in the 52-year history of the U.S. Trials: 235 men and 450 women compared to 166 men and 198 women in 2016. There were plenty of guys capable of making the team.

Plus, I had been pretty silent during 2019 on the racing calendar. I had three uninspiring summer 10Ks, including the historic Peachtree Road Race on the Fourth of July that covered some of the Atlanta Trials marathon course. There were also two 63-minutes-and-change halfs at the United Airlines race in New York and the Rock 'n' Roll in Philadelphia, a disappointing 2:18:56 for 26th place at a more temperate Boston Marathon in the spring, and a somewhat encouraging 2:11:34 for ninth at New York City just four months before the Trials—a mark that broke the U.S. master's record Kip Lagat had set that summer.

But I came to Atlanta more relaxed than I'd ever been in my running life, and in some ways more confident than ever, too. In the interim between New York City and Atlanta, I enjoyed and endured another successful Mudane altitude camp. Gary Lough, who coached Mo and Bashir, was basically coaching me as well. With Coach Murray's blessing, I did the workouts my friends were doing because I knew they would prepare me for Atlanta. Gary was on the bike practically every day, providing encouragement. I wasn't even technically his athlete, but he wanted me to be successful and didn't want to take any credit for it.

When I returned from Ethiopia, Kip asked me how I was feeling about my chances.

"*Watu wataniona kabisa! Watanijua kabisa, bwana!*" I said.

Translation: "People are going to see me, indeed. They'll definitely know who I am, man!"

I feared no one, and I was anxious to get the chance to show what I was still capable of.

🏃 🏃 🏃

CHASING ABDI

From an interview with Carrie Anne Tollefson, Olympic middle-distance runner, on her C Tolle Run podcast, "Abdi Abdirahman: Why Not Me?," March 21, 2018.

Me: As long as you have the passion and the drive and the willingness to be great, the talent's always there. An example like Eliud Kipchoge, like Haile, those are the people that I run with. They might be a little bit younger than me, but someone I've run with, someone I'm friends with, someone I know and I see what he's doing, and I say, for me, why not me? I know I'm not as great as Kipchoge time-wise, but mentality-wise I am. I say, if Kipchoge can run 2:03, 2:04, I still believe I can run a 2:08, 2:07 PR. To this day, I believe I can do 2:07, 2:06 on the right race on the right course. People ask me, so how come you've never run that? I don't run for time most of the time. I don't go to races where there's a time trial or just go to Europe—Berlin—where you just go there for one reason, to run fast. I go to races like New York City Marathon, Boston, Chicago, where it's a pure competition to see how many people you can beat. I like that. I might not be a 2:04 or 2:03 guy, but I beat a lot of guys who have run 2:04 or 2:03 a lot of times.

Time is time. At the end of the day when we lined up, if you want to run 2:03 that day when we lined up, you can run 2:03. But if somehow it doesn't happen, we all run the same time and I pass you at the end, I say, wow, this guy should be sprinting away from me, but he's tired, so hey.

When people see someone in the field who has run 2:03, you should not fear time. You should not fear anybody. If you worry about their time and what they ran, you've already lost the race.

Carrie: Whenever I see you in my mind, Abdi, I see you and Meb Kefleghizi at Stanford. For years, we would all go out there and run those races. You and Meb were chasing each other all the time on the track when you were racing. I can just see you winding up the hand and putting it behind the ear and wanting everybody to cheer on the track. You were always putting on a show. Is that what you feel your role has been in this sport, to make sure people know you're having fun and to get the crowd going?

Me: Yeah, sports is fun. I don't know, everybody is so serious. I remember back in the day, I was running, especially at Stanford or Eugene, I just enjoyed the racing, interacting with the crowd. Maybe I just had so much energy. At that time, I was so young. I just had fun and they gave me energy back.

One week before Atlanta, Mustafa Mohamed had run 2:10:04 in the Seville Marathon to make the Swedish Olympic team. Bashir Abdi was a favorite to win the Tokyo Marathon being held the day after the U.S.

Trials. I was maintaining every day in workouts with Bashir and Mustafa. They were beasts, and our tread marks were all over the rolling dirt hills of Akaki. Why shouldn't I be able to compete in the crowded American race? I also was content in my role as grand old man this time around. It felt good to be the old man, a master's-age competitor still running in the elite class, and to be mentioned as a contemporary of many greats who had retired, as well as other young stars who were just getting started. I had played a part in rejuvenating American distance running in the 21st century; maybe not as dramatically as Meb or Deena, or with singular moments like Ryan Hall or Galen Rupp, or as a visionary like Coach Vigil or Coach Larsen. But I had lasted through it all—whatever competitive career you're talking about, let alone a physically taxing one like professional athlete, to still be among the best in the world after 20 years is an accomplishment to be proud of. The inspiration is in the staying around.

The '80s and '90s were considered "lost years" for American distance running. Since that period, I've represented my country on 13 national teams and been part of prominent performances on the international stage that helped to raise the expectations in my country, including the 2001 World Cross Country team bronze medal, the 2004 Bolder Boulder team victory, and the 2014 American resurgence in Boston. I looked back at all of this before the 2020 Trials not as someone who was contemplating retirement; I looked back at this history and my recent workouts and realized I was in a situation where I had both wisdom and fitness on my side. My past and my present were entwined as one, a calming proposition. No matter how these Trials played out, that's empowering stuff.

I didn't need to look any further than the starting line that morning at Centennial Olympic Park, the hub of activity back in 1996 when Atlanta hosted the Olympics. I stood with a white Nike singlet, white cap, and black shorts, as plain and businesslike as any uniform I've ever worn, ready to get to work. In 1996 when the Summer Games rolled around, that was the last Olympic year I was not a professional runner. In fact, I had put on my work boots and jeans to try out for the Pima Community College team just a few months earlier. A full ride to the University of Arizona was nowhere on my mind. Meb, in front of us now as honorary starter at the 2020 Trials, had just finished his freshman year at UCLA, and I wouldn't have known him if he had bumped into me on the U of A quad in Tucson.

Same with Kip. He was at Washington State then and trying to make a loaded Kenyan Olympic team. He finished seventh in the Kenyan trials and didn't make it to Atlanta in 1996. But he qualified for the next five Olympics, first as a Kenyan and later as an American. Kip qualified for three of those Games in the 1500m—and medaled twice! Now, so many years after moving to Tucson and becoming one of my closest friends, he was a marathoner aiming for an unprecedented sixth Olympic team. He had run his first 26.2-mile race just 14 months earlier. Now, he stood near me at the starting line as Meb shot the gun that sent 235 of us onto the streets of Atlanta.

Our Pac-10 days are long gone, but my memories of Meb and Kip, as well as hundreds of other runners known and unknown around the world whom I have battled against, sweated beside, and laughed with, are deep within me.

🏃 🏃 🏃

With just over six miles to go, Galen was cruising. Maiyo and McDonald were within shouting distance, but this was clearly going to be Galen's day again, as it had been in the 2016 Trials. I was four seconds behind McDonald and laboring. Maiyo and McDonald had exerted themselves as well in the last 15 minutes. I knew I needed to stay close and hope that one of them faltered.

This was nothing like the pain as I hung on those last two miles in 2012. I stayed within myself and maintained my breathing. The 23rd mile, where we dropped off the loop and entered new terrain for the final three miles, changed everything. I moved into second place and McDonald was out of the picture. Korir was back in contention, having caught up to his U.S. Army teammate Maiyo so they could work together to chase me. Seemingly out of nowhere, Jacob Riley had come from nearly a minute back and was lurking. We dropped Maiyo somewhere around the Olympic cauldron—re-lit for the first time in 24 years—and I joined Riley running uphill into the wind, especially stark on the interstate overpass, to try and do the same to Korir. He's fast, and I did not want to have to outkick Korir to the finish. I pushed and pushed on the incline to put as much distance as I could between us.

As we approached Centennial Park, Riley overtook me and Korir was charging only a few seconds behind. The finish line was in sight. Just before I crossed it, I lifted my arms like a bird. And right after I did, I pumped my right fist into the air. I was exhilarated. I found Galen and gave him the biggest hug I think I've ever given anyone. I flashed five fingers to the crowd in the finish area, beaming like it was my first Olympic qualification, not my fifth.

The final times were Rupp, 2:09:20; Riley, 2:10:02; me, 2:10:03; and Korir, 2:10:06. But I was more interested in the story of the race than the times. It ended up not playing out at all like the 2012 Trials. The four contenders going for three spots reset several times in the final miles. It was a tough day on a tough course, and I made sound decisions all the way—to push the pace early, to go with Galen, to attack the hill in the final miles, to be chased and have just enough foot speed to finish where I wanted to be. My wisdom and fitness, my past and present, were all aligned.

When NBC interviewed us, I was feeling a lot of gratitude. I thanked God for giving me health, and good coaching and support that helped me be ready at New York in November and achieve third place here. I gave a shoutout to Galen and Jake standing beside me and said they were great guys. I could have thanked so many more people if I had time: Kip, who finished four minutes back in 18th. My parents, who have sacrificed a great deal to give their kids a chance in America. Diane, who has given me a larger perspective of life beyond running.

I didn't name Coach Murray on television, but he was watching his granddaughter cheerleading at a state championship basketball game in Phoenix when his phone started blowing up. He planned to watch the race later without knowing the result, but he never got that chance. He told me later that he had been thinking about me the whole basketball game, and as it went into overtime, he was glad to know the result so he could focus on the game without worrying about me. Even from almost 2,000 miles away, Coach has never been very good at handling the stress of race day. It's part of what I love about him.

I didn't name Coach Lough either, but I talked to him on the phone a couple hours after the race. He had watched it live, he said, and I remember him being so happy for me. He said he had told some people before the race that he was confident I would make the team.

I don't post a lot on social media, but I guess my hashtags on my tweet and repost of a photo of me wearing the American flag like a cape showed a little attitude along with my gratitude:

🐦**abdiruns**
Thank you everyone for all your support. I wish I could reply to all of you but I am so thankful for your messages and your love
@mudaneteam #Nike #ididit #Number5 #oldmanstillgotit
@coopsrun

I sounded defiant when the *Atlanta Journal Constitution* interviewed me about being the oldest American distance runner to ever qualify for the Olympics and about breaking my own U.S. master's record: "Being the oldest qualifier means nothing to me, to be honest," I said. "I consider myself an athlete. The way I trained for this wasn't a fluke. I put in the work, the sacrifice, the dedication."

I was ecstatic and couldn't wait to get to Tokyo—my record-breaking fifth Olympics and my first in eight years. The marathon was 162 days away and I was excited to get ready. As the "old man," I had no time to waste. August 9 couldn't get here soon enough.

18

THE PANDEMIC
AND BECOMING A CITIZEN
OF THE WORLD

Bashir Abdi left Sululta, Ethiopia, on Tuesday, February 25, 2020, to compete on Sunday at one of the world's most famous races, the Tokyo Marathon.

I had already left Sululta and was in Atlanta getting ready for the U.S. Olympic Marathon Trials that Leap Day, Saturday, February 29. We stay in touch almost every day when we're away from Team Mudane, so it wasn't unusual to get messages from him. He's a lot more serious than I am—about everything!—but it seemed odd when the day before my big race he asked, "How are things in the U.S.?" rather than how I was doing.

"Fine," I said, completely oblivious to what he was really asking.

I knew that two weeks earlier, Tokyo race organizers had abruptly designated it an elites-only event rather than allow some 38,000 runners onto the course. The strange new coronavirus that was spreading in nearby China and around the globe had everybody on edge. Still, Bashir's urgency caught me off guard. It didn't seem real.

He described a lot of Asians wearing face masks on the plane from Addis Ababa to Dubai, which didn't seem all that unusual to me. But then Bashir described arriving at the airport in Tokyo. Everybody was wearing face masks. He and all the passengers had their temperature taken and were given a facemask and warned that they had to wear it everywhere they went. On a shuttle with athletes from around the world going to the hotel, he said the mask made it hard to breathe and he wanted to take it off but didn't dare. At the hotel, masks and hand sanitizer were everywhere. He sent me a photo of him wearing a mask. I barely recognized him with half his face covered.

Bashir isn't someone who exaggerates a situation, so this didn't seem good, but it also didn't seem like the virus was raging out of control. I didn't know what to make of his weird message, but I also didn't worry too much about it. I had a race in the morning, and I needed my sleep.

When I finished my third-place Olympic-qualifying performance on Saturday afternoon, it was almost 4:30 a.m. Sunday in Tokyo. Bashir had his phone with him as the elite runners were transported to the starting line in Tokyo to warm up. He said he didn't see the result until he was about to warm up. "I was so happy for you," he told me later. "I knew how hard you worked in Ethiopia and I knew you could make it, but there were a lot of fresh guys. It motivated me. I was like, 'Damn, if Abdi can do this, why can't I?'"

Bashir did Team Mudane proud, and I'm happy to say he outdid me. He battled two fantastic young Ethiopian runners all the way, finishing in second place to break his own Belgian national record in 2:04:49. It was his third national record in just four total marathons, and he became just the second European to break the 2:05 barrier. Birhanu Legese won in 2:04:15 and Sisay Lemma was two seconds behind Bashir.

He contrasted his last two marathons. After he ran Chicago the previous fall, he remembered going back to the hotel to shower, then returning to walk along the course just to keep the blood circulating. Four hours after he finished, people were still lining the streets, watching the field of 45,000 participants complete their races. In Tokyo, hardly anybody saw him finish. Bashir was quoted as saying, "To start with about 200 athletes in what normally is a race with 38,000 runners was a rather odd experience. It felt as if I was running a tiny street race in my hometown Ghent."

He told me later that when his plane took off from Tokyo to return to Belgium, he thought he was flying away from the virus. By the time he returned to Tokyo for the Olympics, all would be back to normal and the strange day when he ran an outstanding marathon time in front of virtually nobody would be a distant memory.

⚜ ⚜ ⚜

Only after he and I talked again following our mutually successful weekends did the truth of Bashir's prerace message start to sink in. In Japan, which had experienced just one death when it made the decision on February 17 to drastically restrict participation in the Tokyo Marathon, he was hearing more straight talk about the seriousness of the COVID-19 disease caused by the coronavirus. On Wednesday, February 26, the day he arrived in Tokyo, Japan had under 200 cases and its third death. In the United States, we tend to think we are insulated from wars, terrorism, natural disasters, and now pandemics, almost until the moment they arrive at our doorstep. And when those cataclysmic events happen, we believe we will figure out a way to cope with and then conquer them.

This is both a charming and hopeful aspect of the American psyche and also a hopelessly naïve one. We should encourage this type of thinking but temper it with the reality of the world's problems that need serious help from the most powerful and influential country if we are to solve them. Like Bashir, our friends in Asia and Italy especially were trying to shake us into awareness in those early days about what was going to happen. We had an early warning system through them, and we ignored it.

Do you remember that old toy with two big, marble-like balls on a string? I would hold it in the middle and put it into circular motion to try and make the two balls smack each other in midair. When I got a rhythm going, I could make them hit at the top and bottom continuously in a satisfying pattern . . . *clack, clack, clack!* But until I found that rhythm, these two balls would miss, or connect off-center so that they would shoot in all sorts of directions. Sometimes it would come straight at me or crack my knuckles.

When I think about the two balls on the ends of the American clacker—hopeful and naïve—I feel very American. My slow recognition of the coronavirus and Bashir's message is a good example of that. Like many of my fellow citizens, I believe the best is going to happen as long as I take care of myself and those around me and don't get caught up in things beyond my control. It gives me comfort, and it means I don't easily give up. But if I avoid the reality that is going on around me, I don't see suffering in other parts of the world. I think it won't affect me, and in the process I lose empathy for those who are no less or more deserving of pain and struggle than I am. There but for the grace of God go I, the saying goes.

I could have been on a boat that sank before reaching Malindi. My family could have been stuck in a Mombasa refugee camp for many more years. Instead, I've lived a blessed life with choices and opportunities I never could have imagined. I can say it's because I have superior coordination to make the clacker groove, but that's only because I was fortunate enough to get more chances even when the thing popped me in the eye a few times. There but for the grace of God go I. Let's face it: the world got popped in the eye by this pandemic, and we don't seem to be easily learning our lessons.

$$\rotatebox{20}{$\mathcal{F}$} \; \rotatebox{20}{$\mathcal{F}$} \; \rotatebox{20}{$\mathcal{F}$}$$

Almost immediately after I qualified for my fifth Olympics, the world changed. Completely. The day after the U.S. Trials, March 1, the second U.S. death from COVID-19 was confirmed and there were 89 cases in the country. China had reported a total of 2,870 deaths by that time; Italy, 34.

The entire country of Italy went into lockdown a week later. On March 11, the World Health Organization officially declared the global public-health emergency a pandemic, as seemingly every country was reporting cases by the hour. The NBA suspended its season, which shocked Americans, and two days later, the much-anticipated annual

NCAA men's and women's basketball tournaments were canceled. On March 26, the United States surpassed 82,000 cases. By the end of March, more than one-third of humanity was under some form of lockdown.

The fate of the Olympics, which was scheduled to begin on July 24, was discussed throughout March. I was doing interviews under the assumption that the Games would go on—again, I thought we would get through this if people all over the world took care of each other. But the International Olympic Committee met on March 22, and on Tuesday, March 24, IOC president Thomas Bach and Japanese prime minister Shinzo Abe announced in a joint statement that the Olympics would be postponed, "to safeguard the health of the athletes, everybody involved in the Olympic Games and the international community."

Compare that to the statement about the coronavirus that the IOC issued just three weeks earlier, on February 29, the day of the U.S. Marathon Trials: "The preparations for the Olympic Games Tokyo 2020 continue as planned. The IOC is in contact with the World Health Organization, as well as its own medical experts. We have full confidence that the relevant authorities, in particular in Japan and China, will take all the necessary measures to address the situation."

Yep, to put it mildly, the world had changed.

🜚 🜚 🜚

Athletes get asked a lot of questions about world events, politics, social issues. As a Black Muslim athlete born in another country, I definitely hear a lot of these. I fully respect when other athletes speak out about the world beyond their sport, 100 percent. I have strong opinions, too, but often keep the most controversial of them to myself. I don't want to misspeak or have my words misinterpreted. I don't like the negativity that comes with addressing these topics, to be honest. I want us all to get along. I am as forthright as I feel comfortable with and respectful to questions from the media or just in casual conversation with friends and strangers, but I truly just don't want to make people angry.

With the postponement of the 2020 Olympics to the following year, I was in a unique situation shared with only a tiny number of athletes. Few athletes around the world, and especially few Americans whose Olympic Trials hadn't yet occurred, were already qualified for the Games when the planet shut down. It meant those of us who had were perceived as having a perspective that others wanted to hear. That status led to all sorts of questions: Do you feel cheated? Do you agree with the IOC? Are you still training hard? Can you still get the services and facilities you need to train? Do you think athletes should have to re-qualify a year from now to make sure the most prepared athletes are in Tokyo? Are you worried about being a year older when the Olympics are held (I got this one a lot!)? Would you give up your spot? What if you get injured? What are you doing to stay safe? Do you agree with the government's handling of COVID-19? The list went on and on.

While I realized I needed to take these questions seriously and I owed fans honest responses, the more I heard myself and others answer them, the more I realized our perspective wasn't really any more unique or helpful than anybody else's. We were playing a waiting game in 2020. All 7.8 billion of us on the planet. Nothing I or anybody else said was going to change that. My sisters who are nurses could give far more informed answers than me. Teachers, people in the food industry, medical personnel . . . those are the people who deserved to have their voices heard. Or my college roommate Jeremy Lyon. We were supposed to attend a ceremony in Florida for his big promotion in the U.S. Navy just after the lockdown occurred. He continued to do his job serving his country overseas through all of this uncertainty. Doing all I could to stay safe, keeping others safe, and taking care and being compassionate for the most vulnerable and the dead was really the only correct response to any question. Was my training affected? Did I care, given the state of everything else going on?

Remember how Jerry Seinfeld and the cast and writers of his hit show poked fun at the concept of *Seinfeld* by claiming it was a "show about nothing"? The idea was that it was supposed to shine a light on silly, everyday things, and actually, as I understand it from Seinfeld and his co-creator, Larry David, they were quite serious in wanting the characters to not experience any personal growth, any self-awareness, even any hugging, from week to week or season to season. Fairly cynical, I suppose, but it did make for some hilarious television.

What do I write about my life from March 2020 into the early days of 2021, when the pandemic has continued to devastate the world and my country has been divided because of the choices we and our political leaders have made? On the one hand, it's been a year of waiting, where there was little competition and a lot of canceled and postponed lives. If anything, people like Bashir, Mustafa Mohamed (who qualified for the Swedish team after breaking camp at Team Mudane), and I were more fortunate than most people. A lot of athletes hadn't even gotten in one race in 2020 before the lockdown occurred.

It's tempting to call 2020 "a year about nothing." And yet that would be incorrect and a terrible injustice to the tens of millions of people whose lives have been changed forever, often in devastating ways. That's not just the pandemic, either. George Floyd, who died under the knee of a Minneapolis police officer in June, or Ahmaud Arbery, who was shot while running in his Atlanta neighborhood the week before the Olympic Trials, were two of many Black people killed under suspicious circumstances—and during 2020, the world finally took notice and began to admit something was wrong and needed to be addressed. On the other side of the coin, the COVID vaccines were developed in 2020 with incredible speed. That was certainly something to celebrate in all of us trying to move forward.

I can honestly say that as a result of the pandemic and a growing awareness of social injustice, I've learned a lot about myself and how I want to be in the world, including sharing more about my thoughts on politics, religion, and society. It's part of why the idea of a book became important to me, a new opportunity to share the joy and fun I get out of running and life. Maybe it's a chance to inspire people, especially young kids, who—like me as a teenager—don't realize running is an option. Or if they do, they are motivated to make a connection with a professional runner who will be real with them. I want to share my wisdom and knowledge about running, and also help others figure out how to be a better human as I work on that myself.

I envision what I call the Right to Have Hope Foundation as a way to help young African runners get an opportunity to compete and get an education. I see a lot of good that comes from famous people I know—Sir Mo Farah speaks out about racism and the decade-long drought in Somaliland—and famous people I don't know. Bono's ONE Foundation fights poverty, AIDS, and other disease in Africa. I had a run with former President Bill Clinton scheduled one time, but he had to cancel. I would love to take him for a run in Sululta some time and see what the Bill, Hillary, and Chelsea Clinton Foundation could do in Somalia.

Whatever I do, I want to help kids. I love being around them. Coach Murray says I'm 44 years old going on 16. When I walked around downtown Flagstaff in summers before the pandemic, I'd sit down in the front row with the kids and watch "Despicable Me" on the inflatable screen in Heritage Square. When I get requests like I did from Jennie Finch, the gold medal softball pitcher who I know from our University of Arizona days, to send a quick video to her nephew before his state high school cross country championships, I am happy to do it.

CHASING ABDI

Abdi is a man about town in Flagstaff. When you walk around, everybody knows him. It's so genuine. It's not schmoozing. One night I was walking with my parents downtown. They adore Abdi. My dad recently passed away, but he was straight-up hardcore cowboy, rough-and-tumble as they come. They couldn't be more opposite. But he lit up when Abdi came by. He had a special way of talking, trying to talk like Abdi.

—Alicia Vargo, former professional runner,
frequent host when I trained in Flagstaff

Often, I get asked what advice I have for young runners. As someone who didn't start running until I was out of high school, this might seem like a tough question, but it's the easiest in the world to me: listen to your coach, don't get carried away by basing your training on what others are doing, and don't overdo the mileage. Most importantly, have fun with it. If it's not fun, then you won't keep coming back each day. Whatever your body can handle in a workout is just fine. Coach Murray emphasized running as a lifetime sport to his college athletes. He was getting paid to train us to win at an NCAA Division I university, but he didn't want us to stop running when we were no longer his responsibility. Coaches need to do their part to make it fun and not push bodies that are still developing past their limit. Young kids have a lifetime to go on 10-mile runs; they don't have to do them when they are 15 years old.

Gary Cohen, a well-known master's runner and coach, once asked me what major lessons I've learned from my youth in Somalia, the discipline of running, and adversity I've faced. Here's how I answered him:

> Don't take anything for granted in life. Don't overthink about what you want to achieve. It is good to have goals, but don't forget about the immediate things. Young runners may be thinking way ahead to the Olympics, but first they have to go to college and then to the Trials, so they need to be realistic with their goals. Don't live for tomorrow or yesterday, just live today and enjoy what you are doing today. Don't worry about what tomorrow holds. Try to be the best person you can be today at this moment.

What better time to reflect on goals, living in the moment, and the need for unity than during a difficult year like 2020?

ⵥ ⵥ ⵥ

At a time when professional runners had few competitions to stay in shape for and earn money at, The Marathon Project offered a little light at the end of a long, dark tunnel on December 20, 2020. The brainchild of HOKA NAZ Elite coach Ben Rosario, athlete representative Josh Cox, and Big River Race Management's Matt Helbig, The Marathon Project was an invitation-only race in Chandler, Arizona. The flat course offered a good opportunity for runners to get personal-best times, and it gave international runners based in the United States a chance to get Olympic-qualifying times. Prerace talk was that Sara Hall was going to make a go at the American women's national record of 2:19:36 set by Deena Kastor 14 years earlier. The Marathon Project generated a lot of media coverage and buzz. It was a Christmas present for the sport.

Located halfway between Tucson and Flagstaff in the southeast Phoenix metro area, Chandler was an easy trip for me to join the fun. Besides, my girlfriend, Diane Nukuri, was running the race as an ASICS teammate of Sara's. I was there to cheer on Diane and support her along the loop course. Diane and I are both pretty much business when we go to races. Sometimes we'll be at the same race and barely see each other the entire time we're in the city because we have our own commitments, training schedules, and routines leading up to race day.

Since I wasn't competing in Chandler, I saw her race preparation up close more than I ever had. It was a relaxing day for me and a successful one overall. Sara Hall ran the second-fastest marathon ever by an American woman in 2:20:32. Diane, who has been running as an American citizen since 2018, placed 24th in 2:35:56.

But beyond the race results, the day was simply a chance to reconnect with people I hadn't seen much during the pandemic. There was Bernard Lagat, recently named as an interim track and field and cross country coach at the University of Arizona, driving up from Tucson to be a commentator. The race was shown on tape delay by NBCSN and streamed live by USATF.TV. There were participants and coaches from HOKA NAZ Elite, based in Flagstaff. I know their team well. Aliphine Tuliamuk won the women's race in Atlanta the same day I qualified. The men and women whom Ben coaches are all generous with their time and fun to hang out with.

What most people who saw me in Chandler didn't know is that I was injured. I was walking around fine, but ever since midway through a training session on October 4, my ankle was in pain whenever I tried to run on it. I did try to push through at first. Then an MRI showed a stress fracture, which I had never had before, and that scared me a little bit. I had experienced a stress reaction in my femur, but it had never gotten to the point of an actual break. I knew I had to play the waiting game and accept the reality of the situation by resting. Pushing myself too quickly wasn't going to help. My body is like a car, and if the warning light comes on, you've got to take care of it.

CHASING ABDI

When it comes to aging, which has come up with him a lot this year [2020], he has no idea about aging. That's all other people's understanding of what he *should* be doing. I guarantee the only time he thinks of that is when he is asked the question. He spends zero minutes thinking about age. It's not the point to him.

—Mike Smith, Director of Track and Field and Cross Country,
Northern Arizona University

By January, after the inflammation went down and it was clear calcium was regenerating like it was supposed to, I gradually started to run again. At one point, it hit me that for the past few weeks, almost everybody I had talked to was a medical specialist of some kind—in Phoenix, Flagstaff, Tucson, Colorado Springs. I preach patience, but it's not always easy to practice it.

All things considered, the timing was actually pretty good for me. I wasn't missing competition, and the Olympics were still nine months away. A running injury is nothing compared to what others have endured during the pandemic. I had beautiful outdoor spaces in Arizona and an

Olympic spot secured, something my friends on the track didn't get the chance to do in 2020.

Still, I felt the clock ticking even as I recognized my good fortune.

🝔 🝔 🝔

I left for the Team Mudane camp five days before the inauguration of Joe Biden and Kamala Harris as the newly elected president and vice president of the United States. Poet Amanda Gorman spoke her uplifting poem, titled "The Hill We Climb," at the inaugural ceremony, which included these words:

> ". . . If we're to live up to our own time
> Then victory won't lie in the blade
> But in all the bridges we've made
> That is the promised glade
> The hill we climb
> If only we dare
> It's because being American is more than a pride we inherit,
> it's the past we step into
> and how we repair it . . ."

That resonated with me, not just as an immigrant thinking about American society in 2021, but on a personal level. We each have to overcome aspects of our own history, not by undoing those things (which is impossible) but by learning and being better going forward. We do that by welcoming each other into our journeys, into the hills we still have to climb.

A few hours after Gorman's words were heard, on Biden's first day in office, he rescinded through executive order what remained of Trump's travel ban. What would my country be like when I returned from Ethiopia in a couple months? I'm hopeful that my adopted country—my country—is seeking unity again. I want to be part of that effort. As a citizen of the United States and the world, I want to preach it.

Fifth Olympic Ring

Tokyo

There were two Somali-born Abdis on the Olympic men's marathon medal stand—neither was me, but I couldn't have been more proud of my performance or of my Mudane teammates.

Makes sense I called this book *Abdi's World*, right? We're everywhere!

Every Olympics is unique, but Tokyo 2020—held in 2021—was the most unusual of my five appearances. The marathon was held in Sapporo, 500 miles from Tokyo, so it wouldn't be as hot and humid. It still was.

Because of pandemic precautions, I flew into Tokyo after the Games began and went north shortly after, so I didn't attend the scaled-down Opening Ceremonies and barely visited the Athletes Village.

I heard people say how sad it was for athletes not to get a big blowout experience. I didn't see it as negative. This is the world we're in. The organizers did all they could to give the athletes a chance to do what we do best. We should never lose sight of how difficult the past year has been for so many people. Sports is not life and death; a contagious virus is.

I soaked in my Sapporo experience as I did Sydney, Athens, Beijing, and London. It was an honor to be part of this unprecedented Olympics.

Spectators were discouraged from lining the marathon course, but the Japanese have such a strong running culture that we still felt the presence of the many fans who made it to Odori Park on August 8.

Their support meant a lot on a morning that started at 86 percent relative humidity and 78 degrees. Odori Park felt like Sapporo's version of Central Park. Over three loops, we crossed the Toyohira River and passed by the TV Tower, lively (at least pre-pandemic) Ekimae-dori Avenue, and Hokkaido University.

I've come a long way since the first loops I ran around my Mogadishu neighborhood, hiding and then taking the long way around to reach home base. What began as 10 minutes of ducking between houses to elude my friends led to 25 years of running around loops. And here I was, chasing an elusive Olympic medal halfway around the world.

Only 76 out of 106 runners finished the race, a stunning attrition rate for world-class marathoners. But as the incomparable Eliud Kipchoge of Kenya said a few days before he dominated for his second consecutive Olympic marathon gold, "All of us will be in the same frying pan."

That's Eliud: no excuses, no complaints, and a little humor.

I definitely felt the heat but was pleased to reach the finish line healthy. I placed 41st, nearly 10 minutes back. I didn't want a DNF next to my name; a 2:18:27 was the best I had to offer on that day. No regrets.

The excitement was in front of me, as Abdi Nageeye waved to Bashir Abdi—even slowing to urge Bashir on—to follow him to the finish. My friend Bashir overcame a hamstring cramp and passed Lawrence Cherono of Kenya in the final seconds to secure bronze. Though Nageeye is from the Netherlands and Bashir is Belgian, they both left Somalia as young boys, and they worked as a team down the stretch in Sapporo. We all train together in Ethiopia. The trust and strength developed there paid off.

Any disappointment I might have had with my day vanished when I heard what they had done. I spent many years not wanting to recall the conflict in my home country, but now I feel just as happy when my Somali brothers succeed as when I do. All of us on Team Mudane, from Mo to the young guys who will keep it going after we've retired, are a tribute to resilience and love after a childhood of pain and loss.

We all survived a civil war, and in athletics we work together and care deeply for each other. At this point in life, I'm just as proud of being Somali-born as I am of being an American and a citizen of the world.

This book is ending, but my story isn't done yet. God willing, it still has a long way to go, and I'm not just talking about racing. I don't know what I'll be doing a year from now, much less at the 2024 Olympics or 10 years down the line. Not knowing the future makes life fun and challenging. At the end of the day, taking on challenges with joy in your heart is what it's all about.

Epilogue

ON COMMON GROUND . . . BREATHING AND LISTENING

When I go for a long run, I'm taking in and expelling oxygen dozens of times a minute for often more than an hour at a time.

I said early in this book how the beauty of running is that amateurs and professionals participate on the same course on the same day in the same event. My circumstances and yours are probably very different, and I respect your path to getting to that starting line at least as much as my own. But the point is we share common ground when we run, and the analogy continues when we talk about the breathing in and out required to get all of us out the door on a workout, or to the finish line on race day, or really to do any of the thousands of tasks we perform each day we live. You're the same as me; no matter what pace you're going, if your body is in motion, so are your lungs.

Sometimes I crave the company of training partners, to soak up their enthusiasm and their energy and share their oxygen. Other times, I want to explore trails and roads on my own. That's a reminder that we may feel alone at times, for better or worse, but we're also all connected. I know I'm a better runner and person because of the experiences I have with others.

During the COVID-19 pandemic, breathing of any kind, but especially breathing with heavy exertion, could be dangerous to people. The most basic and seemingly simple of all of our bodily functions gave us reason to be scared of what we all could unwittingly do to each other. It gave me pause, and made me more fully understand how much in common we all have. Most importantly, it made me appreciate the responsibility we all have to take care of each other.

Part of doing that is by listening, which sounds like a good idea until we get distracted by our own celebrations and catastrophes and tune out everybody else who doesn't see our side. The pandemic has been an opportunity to see the connection between breathing and listening when it comes to taking care of each other—and taking care of ourselves.

Research says humans spend the majority of our communications in listening mode—and that even goes for people like me who are talking all the time! But let me ask you this: you've been listening to me throughout this book. Now . . . what do you want to say? What do you have to share with the world?

There will be a time when my life isn't dictated by clocks and Garmins and loops. In fact, I'd say in many ways it already isn't. I still get a lot of joy out of what I do, and I'll keep doing it my way. Coming out of 2020, in spite of it all, I'm looking forward to seeing what the future holds and playing an active role in it.

I hope you are too.

ACKNOWLEDGMENTS

When I was on the GoBeMore podcast in the summer of 2020, I told co-hosts Bryan Green and Jon Rankin that I wanted to tell my life story in a book. Jon said at the end of the interview that we had only skimmed the surface and wanted to know when he could read more.

To be honest, at that time I had only been working on it for a few months. My goal was to get it published before the re-scheduled Olympics in 2021. Sure enough, that's what happened, but a year ago I had no idea what that journey would be like.

"I don't want to write just about running," I said to Jon and Bryan. "I'm more than a runner." That was an important point for me to hold onto as the pandemic year dragged on. People in the running community know bits of my life, but this was my opportunity to tell the whole story as well as I could. Other people helped me remember high and low points and details I had forgotten. Writing the book gave me a chance to reacquaint with important people and memories. It energized me during a difficult period, which I know all of us can relate to. The pandemic, injuries, lack of racing, the inability to connect with others . . . this all surely had an impact on what I thought was important enough to put in the book.

I want to thank the many people who helped make this book possible by providing stories, memories, and photos that jogged my memory. These include great friends such as Bashir Abdi, Sean Anthony, Shelley Duncan, Anthony Famiglietti, Bernard Lagat, Diane Nukuri, Mike Smith, Alicia Vargo, and great coaches such as Bob Larsen, Ron Mann, Dave Murray, and Joe Vigil. Most of all, I want to thank my mom, who was willing to recall difficult times in Somalia and Kenya when I was just a boy. If there are factual errors in the book or if I remembered events differently, then I'm responsible, not them.

I'm grateful to Julie Hammonds and Myles Schrag at Soulstice Publishing for seeing my story as worthy of being published. Also thanks to photographers Chris Cooper, Pat Holleran, and Kevin Morris for contributing race photos, and Raymond Suarez at Pima Community College, Mike Christy at University of Arizona Athletics, and Rick Wiley at the *Arizona Daily Star* for finding archived photos that we could include.

I won't try to include all the people I could thank from the past 44 years. You've read about some of them throughout the book, and there are many more friends, family, and acquaintances who have made a positive impact on my life. All I can say is thank you, and I'll do my best to pay it forward.

ABOUT THE AUTHORS

Abdi Abdirahman is the only American distance runner to qualify for five Olympic Games. Born in Somalia, he came to Tucson, Arizona, at age 16 after his family escaped civil war in their home country. Abdirahman became an American citizen in 2000 and has represented the United States as a 10,000m runner at the 2000, 2004, and 2008 Olympics and in the marathon in the 2012 and 2020 Olympics. "The Black Cactus," as the 44-year-old is affectionately known, is also the oldest American runner to qualify for the Olympics, the oldest male to podium at the New York City Marathon, and the USA Track & Field master's record holder in the marathon. Abdirahman is a four-time USATF champion at 10,000m and a five-time U.S. road champion at distances ranging from 10 miles to a half marathon. He has represented the United States five times at the IAAF World Cross Country Championships and three times at the IAAF World Track and Field Championships. He still lives in Tucson.

Learn more about Abdi at his website (**abdiruns.com**) and follow him on Twitter (**@Abdiruns**) and Instagram (**abdiruns**).

Flashing five fingers for five Olympics. Goodbye for now.
(Photo © Kevin Morris)

Myles Schrag is co-founder of Soulstice Publishing and the author of seven books. He holds a master's degree in kinesiology from University of Illinois at Urbana-Champaign and has helped more than 200 books reach publication as either an acquisitions editor, developmental editor, publisher, or manuscript broker.

ABOUT THE PUBLISHER

Soulstice Publishing took root in our mountain town of Flagstaff, Arizona, which sits at the base of the San Francisco Peaks, on homelands sacred to Native Americans throughout the region. We honor their past, present, and future generations, as well as their original and ongoing care for the lands we also hold dear.

Surrounded by ponderosa pines, enriched by diverse cultures, and inspired by the optimistic Western spirit, Flagstaff abounds with scientists, artists, athletes, and many other people who love the outdoors. It is quite an inspiring place to live. Considering the dearth of oxygen at our 7,000-foot elevation, you might say it leaves us breathless.

Learn more at **soulsticepublishing.com**.

Soulstice Publishing, LLC
PO Box 791
Flagstaff, AZ 86002
(928) 814-8943
connect@soulsticepublishing.com

My friend Bernard Lagat
congratulating me on my fifth
Olympic qualifier.
(Photo © Kevin Morris)

The Japan-bound U.S. men's marathon team. *(Photo © Kevin Morris)*